1.35

The Lively Function of the Gospel

The Lively Function
of the Gospel

Essays in honor of Richard R. Caemmerer
on completion of 25 years as professor of
practical theology at Concordia Seminary,
Saint Louis

Robert W. Bertram, editor

Concordia Publishing House, Saint Louis

Concordia Publishing House, St. Louis, Missouri
Concordia Publishing House Ltd., London, E. C. 1
© 1966 by Concordia Publishing House

Library of Congress Catalog Card No. 66-19143

Manufactured in the United States of America

PLANTER

Soil, impatient for seeding, open, warm,
Acres of it in all these years, lay spread
Before you hungry and gaping to be fed,
And some of it a thistled, stony farm
Furrowed by others, rooted and stump-filled —
Yet soil, alive as your hands dug or sieved
Components of life, "a field" as He said, lived
At the edge of your voice, absorbing the seed you milled.
Like Paul, you came, His planter, knowing how
To match the seed to soil, leaving the print
Of wise, of loving fingers on each plant —
Dispersing them blessed and grateful. . . . See them now:
Seeding a million others, they draw rich measure
On measure from that fabulous chambered treasure.

JAROSLAV VAJDA

Preface

The gentle reader will not have noticed: Richard R. Caemmerer's bibliography (pages 191—196) shows that his otherwise prodigious output suffered a slight arrest during the years immediately after he had had most of this book's authors as his students. The only explanation, of course, is that even he, for all his resilience, needed time to recover from the trauma. The least these alumni could do to redress the lean years in his authorship was to write him a book, which does have the one advantage, as their old sermon outlines did not, of sparing him the drudgery of grading. On the other hand, should the suspicion persist in the reader that the authors must have had better reasons for honoring their teacher thus, then no alternative remains but to read what affectionate reasons they themselves advance in their several chapters. I repeat, these chapters are not there to receive a grade. But it is only fair to warn the reader that the authors here show no substantial decline either in the impatience or the zeal which beset them as seminarians.

The dozen authors of this book represent but a tiny and even arbitrary sample of Richard Caemmerer's many alumni. Arbitrary, because the medium here chosen is the printed page (hence most of the authors are either editors or teachers or both), whereas Dr. Caemmerer's chief product is preachers. The most fitting tribute, strictly, would have been a collection of sermons — *viva voce*. Would have been? What else but that has been happening for a quarter of a century all over the world in a million sermons and more?

(Count them.) "Seeding a million others," says Vajda in his dedi-
catory verse, "they draw rich measure/ On measure from that fabulous chambered treasure." ("Chambered," obviously, is an English
pun on "Caemmerer.") At that, the present authors do include
a few — by my count three: Harms, Korby, Lueking — whose style
unabashedly reveals that their first love still is preaching. In any case,
to have to select twelve of Caemmerer's alumni when it would have
been easier to select twelve hundred must have seemed an awesome
assignment to the editorial committee — an assignment they inherited
from twenty some alumni (including some of Caemmerer's present
colleagues) who conceived the whole fond intrigue yet themselves
forewent the privilege of authorship. The twelve who dared, on the
other hand, do speak for all in their unanimous reflection of an old
Caemmerer accent: the lively function, whether preached or printed,
of the Gospel.

In his little theological autobiography, "Stance and Distance,"
Dr. Caemmerer modestly outflanked his assignment and thereby
improved on it. What we had asked him for, as he good-naturedly
complains, was "one of those 'how my mind has changed' things."
What we got instead, it seems to me, amounts to "how my changes
have minded" — minded, that is, like a son "minds" his Father, or
a disciple his Master. The "grand" changes, he notes, were those
which simply extended his initial range of vision, gave distance to the
original stance. From the beginning "the stance has been Biblical,"
but "through the years the Biblical datum . . . has broadened and
deepened." "The stance has not been new. . . . But the distances are
grand!"

These high altitude metaphors and others like them — "the view
from the hilltop," "to stand on a height," "the mounting significance
of the Suffering Servant" — are metaphors you would expect from
a Colorado boy, or from one who has climbed life's hill behind our
Lord. When his son "Rich" mailed in the drawing of his father,
he recalled from boyhood days the morning hymn at Camp Arcadia
and "the vigor with which Dad sang and played" it: "Awake, my
soul . . . and joyful rise." As I can attest, he is still on the rise.
From my "windowlet toward a quadlet" here at Concordia — three
of us on this masthead, though still his students, are now his colleagues — I watch him go bounding up toward the Walther Arch,
never less than two steps at a time. If some of the things we have

written in this book suggest that we in turn have added distance to the stance we once gained from him, that is only a relative observation. The truth is, we are still watching from below. We have much to look forward to, and upward. "But what a view when the fog clears."

Advent 1965   ROBERT W. BERTRAM

Contents

PART I

"But what a view when the fog clears!"

Stance and Distance

RICHARD R. CAEMMERER

When Robert Bertram said "Write one of those 'how my mind has changed' things," my first reaction was: "Isn't that the height of something or other, to be asked to do that?" — the second: "Who will care?" and the third, "Change?"

The first run-through comes up with suspiciously little outright change. The major theological storms in 40 years have been: the nature of fellowship in the church, and the meaning of applying Biblical teaching to life. The men who, by retrospect, shaped my theological stance — Walter Wente, Ludwig Fuerbringer, William Arndt, Frederick E. Mayer principally — had tremendous respect for Christians and Lutherans of many a stripe and tradition; and they practiced, and trained for, a personal integrity in understanding and applying Biblical thought. "Every tub has to stand on its own bottom" was the homespun Arndtism.

The result has been, for better or for worse, that I haven't been comfortable without the Biblical reference, but that I have come up with a series of discoveries through the years that look, by hindsight, like buoys in the stream. Many more men have the same experience. The parallel discovery has been that the Biblical experiences of other men are as precious as mine.

This sounds, on paper, like exegetical exercise. Actually from beginning to end my discoveries have had implications utterly practical.

As a youth my first love was physics and astronomy. It took various forces to lead to studies for the pastorate, the Great Depression to teach insight into the meaning of pastorate, still more palpable forces to direct into teaching and stay there, and to settle for the routines of a practical field by contrast with the congenial disciplines of historical research. Through the years the Biblical datum that has broadened and deepened has been the meaning of *diakonia*. What keeps this from Biblicism has been the mounting significance of the Suffering Servant and His sending of His servants — those whom we teach and those who we are.

Already the pastorate led to exploring the meaning of *agape*, love, in a situation which was wholly applied. The social work people, men like E. G. Steger and E. B. Glabe, produced the breakthrough that people's sacrificial love for one another is not just a pleasant by-product of Christianity, but the very purpose of the atonement; and then the scores of affirmations in the New Testament concerning God's plan and purpose in Christ fitted together. As the years went on, the dimensions of this love, their correlation with the Christian callings, love's reach into citizenship, became plain.

The pastorate initiated, seminary teaching refined the attempt at synthesis of Christian teaching. What is the core? the rallying point? "Law and Gospel," the Confessions had said. But this is an oversimplification, and it depends on understanding "Law" ambiguously — as indictment for which the Gospel provides acquittal, as schedule for which the Gospel provides power. This led to the recognition of a family of expressions in Old and New Testament in which God's presence, gift, supply of life, *zoe,* is primary, to which the Gospel is often applied without reference to the channel of justification by faith. Years of teaching helped to develop the triad of "goal, malady, means" which seminarians distort into sermon outlines and alumni mention with a grin. The education people helped along with the concept of objective and function; the restudy of *kerygma* and *didache* climaxed in the realization that the latter is simply the applying of the former to goals.

Chance requests by conferences opened a trail of discoveries concerning the meaning of the Word of God. I am almost ashamed to admit that the first study was in Luther, but no better way could have been found, I suppose, to catapult into the Bible itself. Here came the discovery that much more is involved than a phrase for describing the authorship of the Bible; that it is God at work; that from Creation to the Last Judgment God is at work toward the world in Jesus Christ; that when the preacher preaches the Word of God he talks words, indeed, but God is acting to produce changes in listeners which He has already produced in the preacher, thus making him a witness; that the Word is preached as the act of God climaxing in Christ Jesus on the cross is proclaimed as an act in time past now applied to action in time present. How sad to listen to men disagreeing with each other about the "Word of God" when they are talking about two different things, and when that which produces power on the heart, the Gospel of God, never is spoken! Again the stance was not different from the years when I heard Franz Pieper say that the power, the efficacy for faith and life, of the Scriptures lay in its Law and Gospel. But the view from the hilltop was farther. A recent stress that has become inescapable is that when the Word of God, or the Christian religion, or whatever you want to call it, is "taught," it better aim always at more than information, although it never employs less than that in the process; it must produce action in faith and/or life.

Over 15 years have dealt with the meaning of the term "church." Again the stance has been Biblical, the concordance on *ekklesia* essential. Most recently has become apparent that *klesis* in the middle of that word is not just a pun; God calls His people out, that they call people out. The postconfessional accent on "visible" and "invisible" had to find adjustment. The agonizing quest for procedure and good conscience in matters of "fellowship" speeded the study. Slowly the realization emerged that the lateral dimension in the body of Christ, Christian toward Christian, was being silenced. A dreadful optimism had prevailed that all was well and perfect in the "invisible church" but that nothing could be done in the "visible" other than that a pastor spoke true doctrine to listeners. Here came greater emphasis on the mission and duty of every Christian to speak the Gospel of God to every other one, and to his world, the pastor serving as coach and trainer; on the worship of the church as the action of God's people simultaneously up to God in adoration, sidewise to one another in the word of edification; on the seminary as a trainer of men who were not to inhabit a status of preferment but a post of service and enablement to God's people. The stance has not been new; both P. T. Forsyth and Franz Pieper had it, in their way. But the distances are grand!

As many another has discovered, the time is suddenly too short. In the homiletical field the New Hermeneutics and logical analysis submit challenges which require intense concentration. Because parish churches in time past have become scarcely able to maintain themselves, the suspicion is abroad that maybe we won't need them in the future. The Consistory in Torgau authorized penalties for moral infractions to be remanded through fines, barely 60 years after the 95 Theses had scuttled indulgences; and we wish that we might look back from 50 years ahead to see our present ineptitudes at diagnosing the ills of our time or prescribing the One Thing Needful or remembering the rock whence we are hewn. The new concerns with a theology of the First Article spur to a mode of restating a theology of Three Articles indivisible. The fashionable words "communication" and "dialog" prod the sluggish brain to present "the fellowship of the Gospel" clearly to our day as St. Paul did to the Philippians. And why, in all the world, don't I take more time to talk theology to my perceptive colleagues, or to Rich and Ray, my sons?

You can get dizzy and a bit afraid to stand on a height in a dense fog. But what a view when the fog clears! Our mutual service in God's church need not be to move each other on to new positions. But certainly we can clear the view from where we stand.

PART II

"... the seminary as a trainer of men who were not to inhabit a status of preferment but a post of service and enablement to God's people."

Pastoral Theology

ROBERT R. SCHULTZ

Richard R. Caemmerer's theological work must be understood in terms of the well-defined sense of responsibility under which he worked. He worked within the Missouri Synod and knew himself responsible for what happened in that group. Consequently, only those who know something of the Missouri Synod as it was 30 years ago will fully understand the extent of his theological contribution over that period of time. The question then was whether the Missouri Synod could make the transition from the 19th century to the 20th without losing the Gospel in the process. There was a fear at the time that it could not, and the danger of its developing into fundamentalist and liberal wings, each with strong moralistic overtones, aroused concern.

Since then the Missouri Synod has passed through a period of massive readjustment. The fact that it has done so without sacrificing its determination to take the Bible seriously as the Word of God and without abandoning its loyalty to the Lutheran Confessions is of no small significance. Many men contributed to this. Caemmerer, as much as any of them, typifies that loyalty and for many of us spearheaded it. He has left his stamp on a whole generation of seminarians and pastors. Caemmerer's work could be described in many dimensions. This essay attempts to indicate the scope of his contribution to pastoral theology.

One hundred years ago C. F. W. Walther published the first

in a series of articles that would later appear in book form as a handbook on pastoral theology.[1] This handbook remained the basis of instruction in pastoral theology and accordingly set the tone of Missouri Synod pastoral work until the decline in the use of the German language and the changing situation confronting the church made a new work necessary.[2] Walther's work shaped the pastors of the Missouri Synod by providing them with an understanding of themselves as pastors and of their work in relationship to the congregation.

Walther's approach to pastoral theology is characterized by the fact that he is more concerned with the pastor as person than as intellect. And he is more concerned with people than with principles. "Pastoral theology is the God-given habitual condition *(habitus)* of the soul which, acquired by certain means,[3] enables a servant of the church to so perform all of the functions appropriate to his office in a legitimate manner that God is glorified and his hearers are saved."

In the following notes Walther spells out some of the implications of this basic statement. He points out that "pastoral theology" like "theology" may be used to designate a type of book or of doctrines. This usage is, however, "figurative and relative." That is, it is true only "under certain conditions" and "accidentally." In order to arrive at the essential and basic meaning of the term, pastoral theology must be defined "subjectively or concretely," that is, as it is found in the person of a theologian. "For this reason, we do not think of pastoral theology as a doctrine or a book . . . but rather as a habitual condition *(habitus)*." [4]

---

[1] "Materialien zur Pastoraltheologie," *Lehre und Wehre,* XI (1865), 97ff. The last article in this series appeared in 1871. They were then revised and published in book form, *Pastorale: Amerikanisch-Lutherische Pastoraltheologie* (St. Louis: Missouri Synod, 1872).

[2] John H. C. Fritz, *Pastoral Theology: A Handbook of Scriptural Principles* (St. Louis: Concordia Publishing House, 1932), p. iii.

[3] Walther refers to prayer, meditation (or study), the temptation *(Anfechtung).*

[4] "Materialien," *Lehre und Wehre,* XI (1865), 97. Space does not permit us to trace the background of this concept in Lutheran theology or its further development in Missouri Synod systematic theology. Cf., however, Walther's extensive treatment of the nature of theology: "Was ist Theologie? Beitrag zu den Prolegomenen der Dogmatik," *Lehre und Wehre,* XIV (1868), 4—11, 72—78, 145—49, 240—45, 265—74, 338—42, 369—76; *Joh. Guilielmi Baieri Compendium Theologiae Positivae,* ed. C. F. W. Walther (St. Louis: Concordia, 1879), I, 32—37, 69—76; also A. L. Graebner, *Outlines of Doctrinal Theology* (Saint Louis: Concordia, 1910), pp. 1—2; Franz Pieper, *Christliche Dogmatik* (Saint Louis: Concordia, 1924), I, 50—57; John Theodore Mueller, *Christian Dogmatics* (St. Louis: Concordia Publishing House, 1934), pp. 33—37.

Walther then further defines this as a *habitus practicus*. The purpose of pastoral theology does not lie primarily in the acquisition of scientific knowledge but in the ability to lead people to salvation through the practice of the church's ministry.

Walther's evangelical conception of pastoral theology ("not as a doctrine or a book . . . but rather as a habitual condition") required an emphasis which was not always easy for his successors to maintain. When an English handbook later became necessary, the work was done by J. H. C. Fritz, whose manual then replaced Walther's as a textbook at Concordia Seminary, St. Louis. Fritz's work depended on Walther's, though not slavishly, and his work is no mere translation either of Walther's words or of his ideas. For example, the opening statement in Fritz's *Pastoral Theology* includes a quotation from Walther: "Pastoral Theology is a God-given . . . practical aptitude *(habitus)* of the soul, acquired *(acquisitus)* by means of certain aids whereby a minister of the Church is enabled validly *(rato)* and legitimately *(legitime),* for the glory of God and his own and his hearers' salvation, to perform all the functions incumbent upon him by virtue of his ministerial office." [5] However, Fritz precedes this definition of Walther's with one of his own, which is not quite the same: *"Pastoral Theology* is theology, or the doctrine of the knowledge of God and of divine things, *applied* by the *pastor,* the spiritual shepherd, to the *spiritual* needs of his flock." [6]

A little farther on, Fritz repeats the same emphasis. He does, it is true, recall Walther's reminder that pastoral theology "does not consist merely in a knowledge of many things, but it is a *disposition* of the soul, which makes of the pastor a sufficient man for the performance of pastoral duties. . . ." [7] However, this statement in turn is preceded by another to the effect that pastoral theology is an "application" of "truths" and "principles": "Pastoral theology, being *theology,* is not idle speculation or a system of man-made theories and rules, but *has its source in the Word of God* and states *the eternal truths* and the *divine unchangeable principles* which should be faithfully applied to the *spiritual needs* of men." [8]

[5] Fritz quotes Walther's definition from *Pastorale.* The changes from that published in *Lehre und Wehre* in 1865 (see above) are slight. However, the addition of "validly *(rato)*" and the explication of *"rechtmässig"* as *"legitime"* point to a development within Walther's own thinking.

[6] Fritz, p. 1.

[7] Ibid., p. 2.

[8] Ibid., p. 1.

Although the influence of Walther upon pastoral theology remained dominant in the German period and by no means disappeared even in the English period, some students find less emphasis on the evangelical principle in pastoral theology during the post-Walther period. The evangelical principle develops pastoral work as an expression of the pastor's own faith as a man and as a concern for the redemption of people. The loss of the evangelical principle through the intellectualization of pastoral theology permits the substitution of knowledge of the code for faith, and the preservation of principles, policies, and the institutions which they represent for the salvation of persons.[9]

Since 1940 the evangelical approach to pastoral theology has been strongly reiterated in the Missouri Synod. Many men have contributed to this spirit, but none has nourished it more vigorously than Caemmerer; and no one has more effectively helped to spread it throughout the church than he did. During the past 20 years those outside the Missouri Synod have noticed the growing concern of Missourians for people.

Caemmerer was deeply concerned that the evangelical pastoral principle be implemented in practice. He helped individual students in his homiletics classes to see the moralism in their sermons and to proclaim the Gospel of Jesus Christ.[10] Caemmerer was one of the signers of "A Statement" and was one of the four men who presented papers to the conference which produced that document.[11]

This awareness is focused in a pre-Lenten meditation on Jer. 5: 30-31 titled "A Wonderful and Horrible Thing." Under the subheading of "The Danger of False Teaching Among the Orthodox," Caemmerer writes:

> The teachers and editors of our Missouri Synod protest against the false teachings which pervade so much of professing Christendom in our time. They will continue to do so. But Scripture calls us not only to castigate false teaching in others, but to be sensitive to the menace of decay in ourselves. Our church protests against false doctrines of justification or of the nature of God and of Christ. The Word of God

[9] *Speaking the Truth in Love: Essays Related to A Statement, Chicago, Nineteen Forty-five* (Chicago: The Willow Press, n. d.).

[10] The implications of such a diagnosis are indicated in an analysis prepared by one of Caemmerer's students. See the unpubl. diss. (Concordia Seminary, Saint Louis, 1952) by William Backus, "An Analysis of Missouri Synod Sermons Based on the Content of the New Testament Kerygma."

[11] Reported by Theodore Graebner, *Lutheran Witness,* LXIV (1945), 323.

calls us, however, to face the danger of false teaching and faulty teaching in ourselves. That danger exists because every Christian this side of the grave bears in him the taint and threat of the flesh, which may blind his vision to the truth and weaken his will to put the truth to work in his life. It is false teaching when the doctrine of the consecrated life is set forth badly; it is faulty teaching, and hence equally false doctrine, when the truth is said well but allowed to be distorted and die in practice. It is false doctrine to describe the content of the Gospel falsely; it is faulty teaching and hence equally false to lead men who have the pure Gospel to be sluggish and apathetic toward the needs of sinful men. It is false doctrine to teach wrongly about love; it is equally false doctrine when, saying the right words about love, people are found in so sad a state that they can despise their brethren. The prophet who speaks the good word so that it dies in the hearer's mind and heart is worth no more than the prophet who prophesies falsely. Let our Church survey the gains which it has made in the last fifty years in Christian charity, in the warmth of fellowship, in the sacrifice for the needs of men everywhere, and then place next to them the words of Jeremiah." [12]

In the next section, Caemmerer describes what happens "When the Gospel Becomes a Code." "Where teaching and prophecy does not bring home to the individual the life of God through Christ Jesus, it shrinks and shrivels to the stature of a mere code of action and body of religious exercises; and instead of producing the very life of Christ in the body of Christ, the Church, it breeds the deadly progeny of carping, life by rule, censoriousness, pride. The people may use godly words and the code and hope to serve God through the exercises, but the Spirit of God is not in what they do." Caemmerer then asserts that the legalism which the Missouri Synod most abhorred and condemned in others could be found in the Missouri Synod itself. These and similar statements by Caemmerer and others alerted Missouri to the disease where it had infected its own practice, and to the need of reexamining and revising its own position accordingly.

Caemmerer's warning against the failure to express Christian confession in Christian life is rooted in his understanding of the Gospel. In an early article, "The Dynamic of the Lutheran Reformation," Caemmerer points out that the power of the Reformation lay in its doctrine of grace and of faith even more than in its doctrine of Scripture, basic as that is.[13] The fact that this statement could be published when the Missouri Synod was on the point of adopting

---

[12] *Lutheran Witness*, LXVII (1948), 38.

[13] *Concordia Theological Monthly*, I (1930), 579.

"A Brief Statement" should serve as a caution to those who assume that the synodical position at that time was exclusively centered in the doctrine of Biblical inerrancy.

This article then, asserts that many Lutherans had partially lost the basic dynamic of the Reformation. That assertion is spelled out much more precisely and clearly in a later article, "The Melanchthonian Blight." In this article Caemmerer points out that Melanchthon at first shared "Luther's vivid insight into the total change which the redemption of Jesus Christ and the presence of Jesus Christ makes possible in the child of God."[14] In time, however, Melanchthon's "Humanistic heritage and . . . educational preoccupation combined to produce the un-Lutheran but potent oversimplification of Christian knowledge as information, apprehended by a mind which is to all intents and purposes identical with the natural mind." Thus Melanchthon intellectualized conversion by making it a process of acquiring knowledge of the facts of the Gospel. Faith then became "the recognition and confidence that God Himself says what is believed." [15]

This brings with it a shift in the understanding of the new life of the Christian. "With Luther the doctrine basic to the new life is the concept of regeneration. The man who is justified by faith is not only forensically approved in God's sight, but Christ works a totally new life, concurrently with the faith. For Melanchthon this link is characteristically limited to an operation in the mind." [16] Luther's practical ethics were centered in "Christian love, which operates in the service which the Christian renders in his calling. Melanchthon abridges this concept and establishes a dynamic for practical living which is not the atonement of Christ, but the sanctions of Law."[17] The analysis struck home to some of us not only as a valid historical analysis of the Reformation but also as a description of the type of Gospel which here and there had invaded the educational system of the Missouri Synod.

Caemmerer concludes his article, "The Melanchthon[ian] blight is insidious. For it operates with terms and definitions that convey, in part, insights and principles essential to the Gospel; and it is

[14] *Concordia Theological Monthly,* XVIII (1947), 327.

[15] Ibid., pp. 328—30.

[16] Ibid., p. 332.

[17] Ibid., pp. 333—34.

natural to the thinking of men who are in the profession of applying
mental processes to the materials of religion." [18] This is specifically
applied to pastoral theology: "A weakening of the fundamentally
spiritual concept of the Christian calling is apparent in Melanchthon's
construction of the nature and function of the Christian ministry." [19]

Caemmerer then proposes two antidotes to the Melanchthonian
blight and therewith sketches his own program for a renewed emphasis on the evangelical spirit in Missouri Synod pastoral theology
wherever it was endangered. The first part of that program calls for
clarification of the fact that the knowledge, death, and life of the
Christian are not simply mental and intellectual categories but that
they are dimensions of his total life. "Another antidote is to realize
the evangelical character of the ministry. That means emphasizing
the sense of purpose and the will to serve people. It means drawing
upon the impulses of the new man in Christ for the functions of the
ministry. It means employing a technique of ministry which recognizes the handicaps and the essential paganism in marshaling people
to a conformity to code, and instead endeavors to bring the propulsion
of the new life through Jesus Christ to bear on men through Gospel
and Sacrament."[20]

The work of Caemmerer is, God willing, far from finished.
What is clear even at this point, however, is that this program has
in large measure been achieved. As a result the Missouri Synod has
the opportunity of moving to a much fuller realization of Walther's
vision of pastoral theology than it had in 1865.

The essay on the Melanchthonian blight was followed almost
immediately by two essays that spelled out its implications for pastoral
theology in fuller detail. The first is an essay on homiletics, "Lutheran Preaching and Its Relation to the Audience." Here Caemmerer
contrasts Luther's method of preaching with the homiletical method
which Melanchthon taught to theologians. Melanchthon, humanist
that he was, emphasized grammar and rhetoric. Luther on the other
hand emphasized dialectic.[21] Caemmerer concludes that although
"the humanistic theory made some useful contributions to Lutheran

18 Ibid., p. 337.

19 Ibid., p. 336.

20 Ibid., pp. 337—38.

21 Ibid., pp. 881—84.

preaching," such as the emphasis on the "doctrinal core" of the sermon, its "Scriptural basis," and the "traditions of careful preparation and thorough revisions of style," yet these did not overcome its basic handicap: "the pastor did not continue Luther's passion for the person." Caemmerer then points out a basic similarity between Luther's homiletical method and the emphasis of modern methods of speech: for example, the speaker sees himself only as a tool and means, and he uses his entire personality to concentrate completely on the hearer. Caemmerer concludes that "the stage is set for a revival of Lutheran preaching in the elemental sense of Luther's own method." [22] This is then developed in his *Preaching for the Church*.[23]

The emphasis on the pastor's concern for the person of the hearer and on the pastor's use of his entire personality corresponds to Caemmerer's emphasis on faith and Christian life as dimensions of the entire personality. Caemmerer in this way reaffirms Walther's definition of theology as the habitual condition *(habitus practicus)* of the theologian which results in action and not merely in thought. "For God Himself has to empower the pastor-bishop for his work, and that takes hold in the heart first of all." [24] This same concern comes through clearly in Caemmerer's book on church administration, *Feeding and Leading*. It is one of the unusual insights of this approach that intimate relationship between church administration and liturgics is recognized not only in theory but also in practice.[25] Both are viewed in the same perspective and considered important in terms of a common purpose.

This approach to pastoral theology places the pastor within the framework of the universal priesthood of believers. The pastor seeks to lead his hearers to be what he himself as pastor is. Caemmerer points this out in the second essay developing the implications of his essay on the Melanchthonian blight for the pastoral ministry, "The Universal Priesthood and the Pastor." Caemmerer writes: "In the exact sense, there is no distinction between minister and layman; the difference is not one of rank or station *(Rang* or *Stand)* but of func-

22 Ibid., pp. 885—88.

23 St. Louis: Concordia Publishing House, 1959.

24 "The Pastor at Work," *The Pastor at Work* (St. Louis: Concordia Publishing House, 1960), p. 13.

25 St. Louis: Concordia Publishing House, 1962, p. 20. Cf. "On Liturgical Uniformity," *Concordia Theological Monthly,* IX (1938), 432—40.

tion and work *(Amt)."* The pastor is always concerned to train people to carry on the same ministry that he does.²⁶

Caemmerer's works on pastoral theology are permeated by this assertion. The book *The Church in the World*²⁷ presents a theology for the work of the Christian in terms of his witness of love and proclamation of the Gospel.

Caemmerer explicitly points out that this understanding of the universal priesthood was very important in the years between the Altenburg Debate and the organization of the Missouri Synod. The congregations themselves fluctuated between episcopalism and congregationalism. The St. Louis congregation "made its anti-episcopal misgivings felt" in the first constitution of the Missouri Synod. "Under the dominating personality of Dr. Walther," however, it reverted to an attitude of extreme deference to the pastor. "The people were trained through the generations from 1860 to 1900 to defer to the doctrine and to the administrative judgments of their pastors. . . . The result was frequently that the doctrine of the royal priesthood was preached and praised, but not realized."²⁸

This corresponds to the development of the understanding of pastoral theology. Walther's definition of 1865 left some possibility of distinguishing between the pastor and the layman apart from their function and office. The habitual condition of the pastor could as easily be found in the layman. The slight revisions of the definition as it appears in *Pastorale,* with the increased emphasis on the validity and legitimacy of the pastoral ministry, reflect the concomitant relegation of the royal priesthood to the realm of theory rather than practice. The potential unclarity in Walther's definition, as it relates to the universal priesthood, becomes obvious as soon as we ask what it is finally that makes the work of the pastor legitimate. Is it conformity to the laws and regulations of the synod? Or is it, as it is also for the work of the layman, first of all conformity to the Gospel?

Caemmerer's analysis of the Melanchthonian blight relates this emphasis on the position of the pastor to the intellectualization of the Gospel. This latter becomes clear whenever the Word of God is thought of primarily as conveying intellectual information and little

²⁶ *Concordia Theological Monthly,* XIX (1948), 569. Cf. *The Pastor at Work,* pp. 11—12.

²⁷ St. Louis: Concordia Publishing House, 1948.

²⁸ *Concordia Theological Monthly,* XIX (1948), 573—74.

more. Caemmerer deals with this problem with great finesse, and the results are clearly stated. There are two major emphases in the Bible's understanding of the "Word of God." One is "the idea of active purpose, the working out of a design and intention; thus the term is synonymous with force, activity." The other is "the idea of communication; the force, purpose, and activity is being registered toward people, made apparent in them or to them." [29]

Caemmerer thus deals with a most crucial issue and deals with it by direct recourse to Scripture. Similar studies frequently appear in his work. It is characteristic of this method that he thus helps the reader to listen to the Bible and permits the categories of understanding to be shaped by the Biblical usage.

This willingness to confront the proclamation of Scripture and to allow it to work on him characterizes Caemmerer's homiletical and pastoral methodology. It is rooted in his conviction that God Himself works through the proclaimed Word and thereby changes not only men's thinking but their lives. Caemmerer comes to grips with the basic issues of sin and grace, both in the Biblical message and in the situation of the people to whom he speaks, in such a way that the words of the Bible take on immediate relevance for the present situation. This dynamic approach to Scripture as the Word of God is presented by Caemmerer — as it was by Walther — in terms of a clear relationship and distinction between the Law and Gospel.[30] Caemmerer's reiteration of this basic concern of Lutheran theology, coupled with a similar emphasis by his colleague, F. E. Mayer, kept this basic theme in the central position in Missouri Synod theological discussions.

On his retirement from the staff of the *Lutheran Witness*, Caemmerer summarized what he felt was happening in the Missouri Synod from 1932 to 1952. It is illustrative of his own practical application of the doctrine of the royal priesthood of all believers that this article — like the call to repentance, "A Wonderful and a Horrible Thing,"

[29] "A Concordance Study of the Concept 'Word of God,'" *Concordia Theological Monthly*, XXII (1951), 171.

[30] Cf. "God's Grace the Preacher's Tool. A Homiletical Study of Titus 2:11-14," *Concordia Theological Monthly*, XXI (1950), 105—12; "The Educational Use of Scripture in the Light of the Doctrine of the Holy Spirit," *Concordia Theological Monthly*, XXVIII (1957), 211—19; "Theology and Love," *Concordia Theological Monthly*, XXX (1959), 241—42; "Kerygma and Didache in Christian Education," *Concordia Theological Monthly* XXXII (1961), 197—208; "Fighter and Friend," *Concordia Theological Monthly*, XXXIV (1963), 581—82.

published 4 years earlier — appeared in the synodical organ (the *Lutheran Witness*) addressed to pastors and laymen alike.

Caemmerer points out that he has seen

a growing readiness to let the Word of God in the Bible speak. Our Synod has always been a group of congregations and individuals who subscribe to the Lutheran Confessions and who taught the doctrines of the Church as they are formulated in Luther's and the synodical catechisms and in the professional books used by the ministry. This trait of our Church was valuable and contributed to the uniformity and clarity of its teachings. One danger, however, was latent in that emphasis and caused itself to be felt particularly in the years of change from German to English parish life. That was the danger of listening to the Confessions and the handbooks and neglecting to explore and recapture the significance, point by point, of the Scriptures behind them. For the Confessions are always to be "a rule that is ruled," namely, by the Scriptures. Only these are "the rule that rules."

It has been good to see the Missouri Synod rising to the challenge of recapture. To the observer from the outside, the significant thing about the Missouri Synod is its parish life. . . . It is good to see that the output of the Word of God in the Bible, from pulpit and in classroom, through worship and other group work, is honestly on the increase.

With this trend we may expect certain discomforts to emerge, and they have come. The restudy of the Scriptures results from time to time in the discovery that our formulations of doctrine have subtly begun to mean something to us other than was their original intention. The formulations of doctrine are simply vessels into which the living water of the Word is poured. The restudy of the Scriptures means that the vessel stands there, not just with a label on the outside, but filled and charged with its original meaning. We can expect men and women to be dismayed from time to time that they have fondled vessels which have been getting empty. The discomforts of these discoveries have marked the past twenty years in our Church. The Holy Spirit, who leads us into all truth, must Himself be the Comforter! [31]

This is how Caemmerer himself describes what was happening in and around him. The historical perspective is too short, his work too far from being finished, to evaluate adequately all that happened. But the very shortness of that perspective makes it necessary that whoever writes about it also describes it from the perspective of his own experience.

Students at Concordia Seminary, St. Louis, during the late 1940s experienced Caemmerer as a man who embodied his theology. He

[31] "Listening Post," *Lutheran Witness*, LXXI, No. 16 (1952), p. 7.

was the pastor of countless seminarians and became one of the channels through which the gift to be something of the same was communicated to them. Someone said — and it was true — that we did not climb the stairs to his office in order to hear the answer but to see it. He was in his own person a pastoral theologian not simply because he taught pastoral theology but rather because he was one in his own person. In Caemmerer pastoral theology was a *habitus practicus,* and he was the pastor of countless students at Concordia Seminary, St. Louis.

His writings are, therefore, only an imperfect documentation of his contribution. The real documents would be the transcripts of the endless conversations — if there are such — and the carefully detailed and theologically penetrating notes handed back with sermons in all their various stages of preparation.

The Missouri Synod was in linguistic transition. Latin had been translated into German and transliterated into English. The old terminology did not speak to many of us. We all used the terms, but few asked what they meant. Caemmerer spoke to us in English and in terms of the world in which we lived. Looking back, it is difficult to recapture the amazement which we felt as we heard the Gospel from him.

In the process his pastoral theology became the central element which integrated all that we were learning and put it into a meaningful context. Missouri Synod scholarship was not always what it might have been — but this integrated what we had and provided us with a good foundation for future building. Caemmerer taught us quite simply that we did not know the significance of what we were saying or doing until we knew its relationship to the Gospel and understood its significance for our own lives. In this context all other theological disciplines took on a new meaning.

This made for a vital approach to preaching. Sermons were constructed not on the basis of syllogisms but on the basis of the inner logic of the communication of the Gospel. He taught us to be pastoral theologians, and in the process we learned theology.

Caemmerer helped us to be concerned about people and about what was happening to them as they lived in the church. He could teach us this because he loved people and loved us. This capacity to love seminarians must surely be classified as a charismatic gift. In this he taught us to see the church not merely as an institution or organization but as people. What seems obvious to us now was not so obvious to us then. Where we exaggerated our organizational loyalties — ranging from loyalty to prep schools to loyalty to the Missouri Synod — or (what often came to the same thing) exaggerated our rebellions against these organizations, Caemmerer reoriented us toward people. The results were evident in the late '40s not only in the life of the student body but of the faculty. *Koinonia* became an experience.

As we learned to see the people in the church in the Missouri Synod, we also learned to see them in the church outside the Missouri Synod. The improvement of our attitudes toward other Lutherans and even other Protestants was a direct result of this.

Because Caemmerer was concerned about people, he shared neither our loyalties nor our rebellions. Standing above them, he did not react to them, but to us as persons. In his presence we experienced the freedom to disagree. He was not defensive about doctrine. We could ask the difficult question: the one we couldn't answer and which he might not be able to answer either. Even when we did not hear the answer from him, yet the fact that he could live with the question and its inadequate solution gave us the courage to do so ourselves. The loyalty of Missouri Synod theological scholars to the Missouri Synod is evidence of the fact that somehow it became impossible to do all the things that the institution said we dare not do and still remain related to its basic concern.

Caemmerer was equipped to do this because he understood the Melanchthonian blight and its threat to Missouri Synod theology. Being freed of this intellectualization and moralization of the Gospel, he was free of the compulsion to affirm or reject a particular formulation as though eternal salvation depended on it. We knew that he frequently disagreed with what passed for the "official position" in those days, but no man was more loyal to the Synod. He could do this without dishonesty because his life was not centered in his relationship to the institution. In this same sense, he was also free in relationship to the synodical fathers. Because he could admit they were not the last word, he was free to hear what they had actually said in their own situation. He was able to affirm their intention and the positive value of what they had done and then to build on it. In this he taught us to be historians.

Caemmerer was a center of growth. Interestingly enough, he

never became a storm center, and neither friend nor foe could make him one. He was simply not concerned about the things most under discussion. He was concerned primarily about people. And his understanding of history lifted him above the questions that we were so hotly debating during the past 25 years (where have they all gone?) to the basic theological issues. In those days when some of us were tempted to vacillate between pietistic orthodoxy and pietistic rationalism, Caemmerer was one of those who continued to point to the Confessions and Luther. In all the great debates, he spoke. But he desisted from answering those questions that were being asked from the point of view of the church merely as an institution. Rather he answered the questions that were ultimately significant, also for the church. It was already a gain when we but learned to ask the questions he was asking.

It is a tribute to Caemmerer, as it was to his worthy predecessors in the St. Louis seminary and in the Missouri Synod, that his contribution there is regarded no longer as unique but as almost self-evident. In some instances he cleared the air so that we could see others who went much the same way independently of him. In other instances his own students have spelled out the farther implications of what he taught them. In many perspectives he can virtually be taken for granted. It is good that it is so. What he is engaged in is the work of the church. In any case, this would have gone on without him, but now it will be done more pastorally in the lives of people. That is, the Gospel will be communicated more meaningfully because of what we have received through him.

PART III

"Here came greater emphasis on the mission and duty of every Christian to speak the Gospel of God to every other one, and to his world, the pastor serving as coach and trainer."

CHAPTER 3

Ministry

F. DEAN LUEKING

As seldom before in the long history of the Christian church, the ministry is undergoing a period of critical scrutiny by concerned people. Let us accept this, not with resentment but with gratitude. There is no quibbling with statistics that show seminary enrollment is sagging. Nor can any responsible churchman gainsay the fact that a majority of the most gifted youth of the church are turning to other vocations than the ministry for their lifework of Christian service. Not irresponsible unbelievers, but utterly earnest believers who love the Lord, His church, and the world for which He died tell us the truth about obsolete forms of ministry in today's church. They point to our metropolitan areas, where maximum ministerial forces are concentrated in locations of minimal influence upon daily life. Rural and small-town America, long regarded as the stronghold of Christian piety, is not a fortress of the faith but is a mission field awaiting those creative forms of ministry that will bring the divine Word beyond the veneer to the heart of life. From every quarter of the church comes evidence of a restless stirring in quest for more effective ways and means for the church to be the channel of God's life to the world rather than a curio on the periphery of things.

There is no virtue in denouncing such stirrings, for surely they signify the gifts of the Spirit who never leaves any age without His witnesses. In short, we are privileged to be living in an age of transition. As long as we are convinced that God has a hand — a loving, purposeful hand — in the changes that we are experiencing and must yet experience in church and world, why panic or throw up our hands in despair? Is it not better to lift them up with penitence and thanksgiving to Him from whom the gift of ministering comes?

GOD CREATES THE MINISTRY BY A WORD

For the gift of ministering shall not be withdrawn from the church by her risen and ruling Lord Christ. He has accomplished the work in behalf of the world given Him by His Father; the cross is the lasting sign that He has conquered all that overcomes us. What has God left undone in Jesus Christ? With what manner of sin is He unable to cope? What wayward will of man or rebellious disobedience from within the ranks of those who bear His name can ever withstand or outlast Him who comes to all things not as a stranger but as Lord, since all things were created by Him and for Him? He has put the full power of His resurrection victory over sin into a word that may be spoken. That word is the message of good news, the Gospel of the forgiveness of sins through the redeeming work of the Son of God. Through that word comes the empowering gift of the Holy Spirit which creates the ministry. Ministry means service, God's own service in the name of Him who came not to be served but to serve by giving His life as a ransom for many. The reason, then, why ministry is not going to disappear is that God is not going to disappear. His heart is turned with favor toward the world which has not earned it. His mercy is meant for every man.

GOD GIVES THE MINISTRY TO THE LAITY

And now to the question which is so crucial for ministry today: To whom does God give the gift of joining Him and working with Him in His ministering to the needs of human beings now? Who are the ministers? The New Testament has a very clear answer for the question: all of God's people. The ministry is given to the whole body of believers. The word *ministry* is not limited to a special group of people with particular gifts and training. That special group, which would include pastors, teachers, evangelists, prophets, et. al., has the assignment of supplying the laity with what they need to carry out their ministry of service to God in the church and world. Eph. 4:11-12 is one of the clearest New Testament statements on the subject: "And these were his gifts: some to be apostles, some prophets, some evangelists, some pastors and teachers, to equip God's people for work in his service, to the building up of the body of Christ" (NEB). As we take our cue from this Biblical source on the meaning of ministry, this is the picture that emerges: God's saving will toward the world is revealed through the Gospel of Christ Jesus, a special corps of messengers of that Gospel is called into being by that very word of forgiveness which has found a home in their own hearts, and this special corps lives and works for the purpose of equipping God's people, the laity, for their work of ministering in His service.

What happens when we measure our present ways of thinking and doing in regard to the ministry by this Biblical pattern? The first thing that is obvious is that we have attached the word ministry to the small, special corps of pastors and teachers instead of to the whole body of believers. This is more serious than a matter of semantics. As long as the laity thinks of itself as a passive group of people whose chief function is to support and maintain the professional workers in the church (whom we all call ministers), the full, vibrant meaning of ministry will be shriveled down to a mere caricature of what God means it to be. Likewise, as long as a special corps of helpers in the church think of ministry as the sum total of their own activities, the inclusive purpose for which God appointed them as pastors and teachers will not be realized. Whenever a special corps of helpers take their eyes off the Word which gives them their being and off the whole people of God for whom the ministry of that Word is intended, tragic consequences follow. Then pastors begin quarreling among themselves for prestige and preferential standing. Then comes bickering among church administrators for the limelight, and teachers carry on the lament that their salary is lower than the preacher's.

Or if such things seem to be overly harsh, then the consequences can take other forms. The most common malady of the pastoral corps of servants today seems to be nervousness and uncertainty because certain traditional forms are coming under judgment and passing away. The obsession with one form of pastoral work — let us say, the residentially based parish, where everything is measured by the numbers of people inside the church building each Sunday and the budget potential they represent — is a persistent symptom of the

problem which a special corps of workers create for themselves and
for the larger meaning of ministry. The forms through which the
Spirit works through His people in the world are not forever fixed
in any single parish pattern. They must change and adjust with every
generation of Christians which takes seriously God's call to minister
in this world.

What is permanently fixed is the function of the Word. It is
through the Word of God that special helpers are cleansed of their
own sins of pride and lovelessness for one another. The Word at
work in their own midst unites them in the harmony of Christ's love.
That very harmony itself is a part of their tools for equipping God's
people for ministry, for it represents the claims of Christ coming true
in their own lives. It is the Word which keeps the special corps at
their posts of service to the laity. The Word builds that unbreakable
bond of love between clergy and laity, and enables the former to
rejoice in the latter as the full work of ministry is carried out in the
fellowship of the faithful and out beyond the church to the world.
These are very large claims indeed, but they have a way of coming
true as the Spirit gives people the heart and wit to put the Biblical
meaning of ministry into practice today. Where may we look for
its signs?

THE SPECIAL TASK OF SPECIAL SERVANTS

A good place to start is with the special helpers, the people
whom we commonly call ministers. In many of the current portraits
of the church which include "warts and all," the pastors, missionaries,
teachers, chaplains, and denominational administrators do not come
off too well. The general complaint seems to be that the energies
of these worthy people are spread in too many directions at once.
As macerated, other-directed, back-slapping, fund-raising parish direc-
tors they either do not have time or will not make time for their
primary purpose: delivering the Word of God to people who will
hear and obey. The complaints are not out of order, and the most
effective complainers are most often from within the pastoral ranks
themselves. But too often the lingering error bobs up again and
again: Ministry is limited to the activity of the paid seminary gradu-
ates who are ordained. The function of the Word delivered in its
fullness to the ministering *laity* is not clearly and emphatically stated
in so many current analyses of the ministry, at least so it seems to this
observer. Indeed one might conclude from some current writings

on the task of ministry in today's world that the special corps has fulfilled its purpose by grasping the dynamics of the cultural context and informing the faithful of their duty over against slum landlords, suburban smugness, the Radical Right, antidemonstration demonstrators, etc. What undoubtedly continues into the present from former days in the Western world is the picture of the clergyman as one who has considerable voice in how things are managed in the world. So often the model for the functioning minister seems to be the man for whose sermons the presses do wait, the executives, legislators, and judges do listen. Because this is rarely the case today, the conclusion is too easily reached that the ministry is an irrelevant relic of a bygone day.

The worst possible thing for the special corps of workers to do in such circumstances is to retreat into a shell or simply give up. Instead, they must heed the Biblical message which connects ministry with the work of service which the laity does. The laity needs no prodding toward decisive places of influence in so many areas of life today; it is already there. As God's called servants do their job well in supplying the laity with His will and Word, it is the laity that is the leading edge of prophetic, priestly, and regal discipleship. The clergy not only has the right to expect this of the laity but the obligation to expect it as the awesome power of the love of God is released through lives of commitment in the world. And the laity likewise can expect that what its servants in Christ say with their lips produces a distinctive way of working together as servants of the Word.

No congregation oriented in the Scriptures wants a pulpit prince who guards his privileged status with a jealous eye. Clergy who measure the ministry by their own press notices are utterly useless to the cause. Above all, the gathered body of believers cannot bear the sight of Christ's servants pulling in opposite directions. What counts is the clusters of parish servants who hold together in the bond of love which the Spirit creates. Such servants form the nucleus of the Christian body in that place. What an immense victory God achieves as He teaches the pastor, the professor, the teacher, the denominational administrator, the missionary, the chaplain, and every special servant in the church "not to think of himself more highly than he ought to think," but to speak the truth of the Gospel to his fellow worker in the genuine spirit of love, to honor, respect, forgive, admonish, sustain, and enjoy his brother! Such a harmonious partnership where each serves to bring out the best in the other is a most precious gift because Satan spares no effort to divide and destroy those who supply the Word to God's people for their ministry. Satan is experienced in tampering with holy things, as the temptations of our Lord make clear. One notable detail about the New Testament account of our Lord's strategy in sending out His own corps of 70 workmen is that He sent them out two by two, not singly. Likewise Paul never went alone, but always in the company of a number of fellow workmen from place to place in his missionary journeying. The lesson must not be lost on us. The equipping of the believers for their work of ministry requires a team of suppliers. At least two must be at it, in order to reinforce what they say by what they do.

Hopeful signs of this corporate obedience on the part of special servants comes from many quarters of the church today. It is not surprising that the most appealing examples of mutual serving come from those frontier edges of the church's life where the demonic realities of a hostile world press hardest. Campus ministries come to mind in this connection, as well as pastoral service in hospitals, homes for the crippled in body or mind, prisons, military chaplaincies, and missionary vocations, both close to home and overseas. In such settings the serving corps is under few illusions that only scattered pockets of unbelief, pain, suffering, and despair remain for the Christian forces to sweep into oblivion. Here the world that is set against God is laid bare, and therefore in these very places the power of the risen Lord is often best known and most faithfully celebrated by His servants. I learned of an inner-city corps of workers who share not only their spiritual witness but their means of income in a common treasury. I heard of a group of special workmen preparing for creative ministry in the city describe their day. What they could not do without was corporate worship each day; the only hour when they could all gather around Word and Sacrament was 6 a. m. (I always thought it was only Roman Catholics who were up and in chapel at that hour!) In isolated outposts of frontier Christian service both in rural America as well as overseas, it is often a faithful spouse who is the partner in speaking the healing Word and opening up to the other the gladness of the Spirit's presence. At conferences and retreats overseas especially, the sheer fact of coming together for a brief time of mutual refreshment and spiritual reinforcing is a privilege which few missionary families take for granted. A keynote to the genuine spiritual substance of such gatherings is often in the offering of intercessory prayer for one another's particular needs as well as for the laity as they bear their witness to those who still remain outside the circle of faith.

Anyone who thinks of these servants and their charges as somehow inferior to the stabilized forces of the home church is missing a large point. They have much to teach their brethren who sent them forth! In what we are accustomed to calling average congregations at home and which, on the surface, may not appear to offer much dramatic encounter with the principalities and powers, there are abundant opportunities for the parish to come alive through a faithful corps of clergy, teachers, deaconesses, parish workers, and other special helpers for the congregation which is faithful in serving one another. A key to this is most often the pattern of staff worship. If there are no regular gatherings for spiritual intake, how can the outgo be at full tide? But when the Word is prized and its power attested in mutual witness of word and deed, then the Spirit is given open access to creative and effective use of those persons who equip the believers in that place. The lines of mutual edification need opening in group worship at least once a week, and growing numbers of parish staffs find that time set apart for retreats in the course of a year means added enrichment and growth in those fruits of the Spirit which are essential in serving others: love, joy, peace, patience, kindness, goodness, gentleness, faithfulness, and self-control.

Corporate worship, genuine witness in mutual care and understanding are not optional for the serving corps. No member can carry out his calling alone. The impact of one life in Christ upon another and the corporate witness of the called servants upon those they serve are essential parts of equipping God's people for ministry. It is an indestructible sign of the in-breaking of that fullness of God's plan for His people which His Son shall reveal in His promised return in glory to consummate all things. It is the responsibility of the pastor to see to it that this evangelical spirit prevails among all those who serve Christ's people.

I covet for every servant of the Word an experience that came to me on the day following ordination and which reiterates the emphasis of this section of the chapter. As an assistant pastor of 24 hours' experience, I walked into my senior pastor's study for our first

formal session together. He asked me to be seated across the desk
from him, leaned forward, fixed his gaze full upon me and said
with an even voice: "Now there's one thing I want you to keep
straight." In the pause that followed I seemed to sense all my newly
sprouted feathers being plucked (having come from Professor Caemmerer's classroom only a few months before!) as I braced myself
for the blast. "We're not claiming to be doing God's work around
here as best it ought be done," was the sentence that followed, "and
we not only welcome every creative idea the Spirit gives you — we
expect it!" Thus began a matchless privilege of mutual service under
Dr. Otto Geiseman, who now enjoys the peace of Christ while we
march along on this side of eternity endeavoring to help each other
help the flock of Christ.

Equipping God's People for Ministry

The special servants of God's people gather together around the
Word of life and live from it in order that their assignment of connect-
ing Gospel and people might be carried out in full. The lines that hold
pastors, teachers, and the other special helpers together are extended
to embrace all the baptized and to prepare them for their varied
work of ministry. What may be said about those lines that link pastor and people, teacher and class, chaplain and patient?

In reviewing the many settings in which the process of spiritual
equipping takes place, the place to begin is where most of us are
most familiar and which therefore we are most likely to take for
granted. The Sunday service of divine worship is a major opportunity
for serving the Spirit's purposes, but an opportunity that will be
largely unappreciated if approached by either pastor or people with
low expectations. But when a laity is trained to expect great things
because they prepare carefully for worship and know that their
pastors, organist, and choirs do the same, real space is made for the
Spirit. Increasing numbers of congregations are turning to the practice of preparing people for worship by distributing special brochures
explaining the dynamics of the liturgy, also worship calendars which
encourage home and private worship during the week to center
around the Scripture lections, sermon texts, propers, and hymns for
the coming Sunday. In some parishes the whole cycle of adult
instruction for confirmation is based on the Sunday liturgy; what
could be more sensible than unfolding the fullness of the divine

Word along those lines of formal worship which are followed week after week? Such little things as carefully preparing the Sunday morning bulletin to be a real guide and commentary on the worship of the day help accentuate the liveliness of forms which are left to atrophy only by deliberate carelessness and inexcusable neglect.

Here and there throughout the land a pastor will provide the congregation an opportunity to experience the fellowship of the Eucharist in a new and forceful way by re-creating the setting of the primitive church. It always seems strange and even somewhat out of place to precede the Lord's Supper by a potluck supper, and with the aroma of ham and potato salad still in the air to clear the tables in the church hall, then to have members bring forward the bread and the wine for the consecration and the distribution at the very tables where their bodies were nourished. Such practices require care and preparation, but the corporateness of the Christian fellowship in Christ at His altar is more lastingly vivid after one such experience. Furthermore, such opportunities to receive the same divine gift in a different setting help restore the lost sense of joy in the celebration of the Sacrament. After all, it is the resurrection that is celebrated, not the melancholy recalling of a great but dead man! If the Corinthians suffered from the wrong kind of hilarity at the *agape,* perhaps our suffering is from a doleful solemnity that would make an honest smile seem irreverent in the presence of the resurrected Lord! Again, the same "fringe" ministries on campuses, mission frontiers, and inner-city storefronts are places of the most creative renewal in both practice and meaning of Holy Communion as the basic, integral, joyful action of the people gathered for the worship of God and the building up of one another.

In regard to preaching it is well to recall one man's statement of the situation: "It is not preaching, only *my* preaching, that is in trouble." There will never be any substitute for hard work and disciplined habits in gaining meaning from the text and setting it forth with persuasive clarity to those who must have the Word to get on with their daily ministry of service. In this sense, the preparation of the sermon has its solitary side, wherein the preacher has uninterrupted time for work and reflection upon the text and for refining the ways of saying the truth so that clichés, cluttered thoughts, and needless padding are eliminated. But in another sense the whole round of daily contacts with people is a part of the preparation for preaching the Gospel to the needs of God's people so that they may minister to each other and to the world. Wherever and whenever preacher meets people, both believers and unbelievers, the stage is set for listening and learning and understanding better what the flock faces day in and day out. But more significant things happen when the preacher invites the laity to have a share in the preparation of the sermon. Some pastors have established the practice of opening their doors to all who will come, especially the outsider to the faith, one night a week for the purpose of opening the Word in such a way that its message reaches its target with a minimum of roadblocks which mortals put in the way. This method has been used extensively by worker priests and evangelical pastors in Europe, who find so many who absolutely will not come near the church building on a Sunday morning. On this side of the Atlantic there are those heartening signs in scattered places where pastor and elders or pastor and all interested parishioners toil together on the text to the end that the final output from the pulpit be offered with maximum directness to the lives of the laity. It is a universal experience that wherever such methods are practiced faithfully there is a coming-alive of new awareness of the preached Word as the vehicle of the Spirit's power. The truth is heard as truth *for me;* this is the essence of equipping the believers for ministry.

In this connection, it is the wise preacher who responds to a well-meant, "Fine sermon, Pastor!" at the church door with an equally earnest, "Sincere thanks, but it's too early to tell!" What must happen is the translation of liturgy and proclamation into the daily decisions and actions of life. The home, office, factory, and school are the scenes of the real test of preaching. For most frequently the stage is set for the key question to be put to the Christian by the man who stands outside the rule of God in Christ: "What makes you tick?" Then follows the true fulfillment of ministry, when God's man can freely explain his manner of life by words which point unmistakably to the risen Lord.

MEASURING THE MINISTRY TODAY

Is it happening? Is the world being effectively engaged by the whole people of the living Christ? Here the answer must be given with care. On the one hand it is so tempting to simply recount one's most sterling pastoral experiences of the past month or so and conclude that all is well with the church in the world. The other side of the temptation is to look at the shrinking percentage of Christians in relation to world population, the vast zones of human life which have fallen under the Marxist sphere, the other zones which worship affluence, and then come to the conclusion that all which remains to the church in its present forms is the funeral. In between these two distortions lies the narrow way, the hidden life of God's people which both flares out in splendor here and there, now and then, and at the same time groans in travail under the grievous burdens of sin.

St. Paul is a worthy guide, for his epistles begin with praise and thanksgiving for believers, whom he also admonishes and chastises for flagrant sins in the same letter. Hence it is not too sanguine to say an unequivocal *yes* to the question as to whether ministry is going on in the world. Here are signs of the laity ministering, and surely every reader can extend the list both in length and depth. A widow takes in her handicapped mother and tends her bodily and spiritual needs around the clock. Three housewives volunteer a morning a week at the maternity ward of a large charity hospital simply to give the service of love and affection to the 60—80 babies that are abandoned, abused, and unwanted. A premed student takes a year out of university training to travel to a medical mission post in India. A 30-year-old victim of multiple sclerosis, deserted by her husband after she lost control even of the movements of her eyeballs, can still sing softly the great hymns of Easter and tell her fellow patients in halting, pitiful speech, the good news which is still exceedingly good. A real estate agent risks his means of livelihood to house a deserving family whose skin color differs from all their new neighbors, but he accepts the risk because he believes the recruited forces of the God of Amos and Micah and Jesus Christ can withstand the tide of ignorance and cowardice. A lawyer is beaten down again and again by the massive odds of graft but keeps on chipping away because he is convinced that each little effort offered in faith is a consequence of the resurrection of Him who reigns in the world as well as church. A little boy prays to God nightly for all the people and animals in the whole world. A corporation president personally oversees the merging of several companies to make certain that no man near retirement is cut off without a job and lets his evangelical reasons be known in a note to all the employees. A young graduate student takes all invitations to campus cocktail parties, not only to enjoy God's gift of vine and grain, but more particularly to drop invitations to the monumentally bored fellow guests to a cell meeting for study of Word and world. A couple take into their home a troubled teen-ager from a broken marriage and help her find the stability which the Gospel of peace affords. A woman trains nurses and orderlies for state mental hospitals and carries with her a radiance that only the Spirit gives and which enlightens the drab, hopeless atmosphere of lives permanently enclosed in the night of mental illness. A couple somehow hangs on in faith to withstand the waves of bitterness and remorse that assault them after their foster son of 15 runs away from home for the third time to a life of crime.

And so the list goes. But what it really signifies to the eye of faith is not mere isolated instances of hope and goodness in an other-wise abandoned world. These are but surface signals of a deeper network of God's own mysterious working in His world. These are the hopeful omens of that final, complete victory which shall come only with His coming again. Blessed are the parish servants who live close to such signs! Let them rejoice and be glad, for these point to that great groundswell of divine mercy which breaks surface just often enough to keep us all working in hope.

The Decisive Function That Determines Every Form

In this day of much scrutiny of traditional forms of getting the Word through to God's people for the work of ministering, the pas-toral office is all the more privileged a place to be. For here one is enabled to follow that leading of the Spirit with the people who do man the forward positions where church touches world — the laity, who can bridge the chasms which separate the church from effective ministry to today's world. We are just at the threshold of an era in the church's life when some of the best of her servants are learning firsthand the excitement and complexity of the urban world to which the church is called to minister. With the prospect of more Asian and African countries refusing entrance to American missionaries, the church is being forced to rethink her mission along the lines laid out in the New Testament. The ministry belongs to the laity; never before has that simple fact been more decisive for the world-outreach of the church. Therefore the special function of supplying the spir-itual means for God's people and the work of ministry becomes more crucial in every parish. An ugly incident of racial violence in Chicago today is on tomorrow's broadcast to listeners in Stanley-

ville or Djakarta, and it requires so many words and works of healing
and reconciliation overseas to offset the damage done by Stateside
failures in discipleship. It is no longer permitted for us to confine
our awareness of ministry to local boundaries. Whether we like it
or not, what is happening in the local scene can have reverberations
that encompass the far reaches of the earth. The goal of ministry
is faithfulness in Christian obedience where one lives out his calling
between Sundays, and it may just happen occasionally that the mass
communicators will turn in interest and will report to the world
on those things which in a mysterious way undergird the world and
keep it from flying apart at the seams. It is life's first privilege to
be at the supply lines which feed God's righteous men and women
who uphold the world by ministering to it in the name of its Lord.

This chapter has emphasized the lively function of the Gospel
in drawing together the special corps of workmen of God (pastors,
teachers, etc.) into a purposeful harmony of service to those who
are given the gift and task of ministry — the laity. This lively function is what counts, and we may both gratefully receive the forms
of ministry which the living Word has fashioned in earlier days of
the church and sit loose within its present forms as we ever seek
anew the fresh wineskins for the new wine of Christ's grace. In
stressing the importance of the special corps (building each other
up in the Word) and the purpose of the special corps' existence (the
laity), I am echoing things which Richard Caemmerer has said with
much greater clarity and persuasiveness for a quarter of a century
to hundreds of young men who are now scattered throughout the
world. I speak for that scattered brotherhood when I say a heartfelt
word of thanks to our teacher and add the prayer that God will grant
him health and strength to keep on supplying the suppliers for many
years to come. Knowing him as we do, the best form our gratitude
can take, and really the only form with which he is comfortable,
is to say quite simply: The tools you have given us help us see God's
great plan more and more clearly, and there are no words to describe
the joy and blessing of serving His people as they find their place
in His plan both for time and for eternity.

"When the preacher preaches the Word of God he talks words, indeed, but God is acting to produce changes in listeners which He has already produced in the preacher, thus making him a witness."

The Gospel as Preaching

PAUL W. F. HARMS

"Woe is unto me if I preach not the Gospel!"

For the preacher that is like saying, "Woe is unto me if I cease to breathe oxygen! Woe is unto me if I cease to eat and drink!"

Yet on one occasion a pastor chose as his lection this very reading, "Woe is unto me if I preach not the Gospel," chose as his text, "I am made all things to all men that I might by all means save some" — all without preaching the Gospel. One would think that surrounded by Biblical material of this caliber and being Lutheran in background and training, the preacher could not miss. Yet he did. He could not have missed the point more with a text up-dated to read, "Woe is unto me *if* I preach the Gospel!"

The ease and the frequency with which preachers failed totally to speak the Gospel or spoke it only in crippled fashion was demonstrated in a study of some 200 sermons by various authors published over a period of years and chosen by a random sampling method. The author of this study listed eight elements as basic in the kerygma. The eight included such items as: the death of Christ on the cross; the death of Christ had to do with human sin; the proclamation of the resurrection. When compared for content with the New Testament kerygma, a shocking number of the sermons clearly had no Gospel, made no reference to any of the eight items, not even the three obvious elements listed above, and a majority of the remainder of the sermons were, at best, sketchy in this regard. The sermons analyzed were the products of Lutheran tradition.[1] Both these factors intensify the claim that the church fails to speak the Gospel more frequently than it realizes. To claim that the distinctive task of the church is to preach the Gospel is not to say by that statement that it does preach the Gospel.

THE PREVALENCE OF NON-GOSPEL

"There are men, good Christian men, Christian preachers, who celebrate the sacraments, confirm well-indoctrinated confirmation classes, preach nice 25-, 30-, sometimes 35-minute sermons, but they do not speak the Gospel." [2] Addressed to seminarians in a first course in homilitecs, we could take that statement in stride. Spoken as it was (and is) to the ranks of leadership in the church, this statement shocks. Failure in almost any other category of the ministry might be expected and readily accepted in keeping with failures common to mankind. But failure in the heart of things, failure to speak "the one thing needful" — that is disturbing in the extreme. Of all failures attributed to preachers and preaching, none is more serious than that of failing to preach the Gospel.

"Here again the reminder is in place that any active and pleasant man, preaching any mildly helpful and cheery message, can anywhere gather a group of people with a moderate amount of leisure and the normal hunger for companionship into an organization. The fact that people respond to the invitation to found and build a church is not necessarily associated with Christ." [3] Any kind of response coming under church auspices dare not be tagged indiscriminately as a victory of the Gospel. Success evaluation based on an increase in cabbage head count may mean nothing more than an increase in cabbage heads.

"Let us face that fact that it is possible to establish large and strong churches and to do a good job of community organization without at all bringing the actual Gospel to bear upon the membership of the Church or upon the community. The threat of materialism to the Church, then, is not merely that it makes the world impervious

1   William Backus, *An Analysis of Missouri Synod Sermons Based on the Content of the New Testament Kerygma* (Unpublished Master's Thesis: Concordia Seminary, St. Louis, 1952).

2   Richard R. Caemmerer, "The Gospel to Be Preached," *A Symposium of Essays and Addresses Given at the Counselors Conference,* The Lutheran Church — Missouri Synod, Valparaiso, Ind. (September 1960), p. 87.

3   Richard R. Caemmerer, *The Church in the World* (St. Louis: Concordia Publishing House, 1949), p. 96.

to the Gospel, but that it dilutes the Gospel and that it replaces the Gospel with worldly tools and makes the world instead of Christ the goal of the Church."[4] The Gospel diluted, the Gospel replaced till that time comes when Christ and His Gospel are no longer the goal of the church. Now mind you, the board of elders do not sit down and make a formal recommendation to the governing body of the church that the Gospel be replaced. Protests and impeachment proceedings would be the response. But the Gospel can be replaced, nevertheless, by the far more subtle process of dilution. Over the years it gradually ceases to be what it once was.

St. Paul, writing to the Galatians, stated the problem this way: "I am astonished that you are so quickly deserting Him who called you in the grace of Christ and turning to a different gospel — not that there is another gospel, but there are some who trouble you and want to pervert the Gospel of Christ. But even if we, or an angel from heaven, should preach to you a gospel contrary to that which we preached to you, let him be accursed. As we have said before, so now I say again, If anyone is preaching to you a gospel contrary to that which you received, let him be accursed." (Gal. 1:6-9)

We would be horrified, and properly so, if a Christian preacher, for the sake of variety if nothing else, were suddenly to recommend Buddha, Marx, or Confucius. That would be to recommend another gospel. Horrified by the substitution of Marx for Christ, we can be quite complacent about the recommendation of nothing at all. But is not the failure to recommend the Gospel just as horrifying and more debilitating, though not so obviously, as to recommend another gospel? In fact, to recommend nothing when one could have recommended this Gospel is to recommend another.

The Menace of Non-Gospel

A failure to speak the Gospel should draw no less condemnation than the advocacy of a contrary gospel. The failure to speak it at all, especially under preaching auspices, may have greater negative consequences both for the speaker and for the listener than the outright recommendation of another, for both speaker and listener believe that all is well. Meetings would be called, petitions would be circulated, headlines would be plentiful if a preacher advocated the equal

4   Ibid., p. 34.

validity and reliability of Christ, Lenin, and Coué. Yet how often is a pastor called to task when he fails to speak the Gospel? A failure to contradict the atonement does not mean that we proclaim it by default.

Writes Werner Elert: "For whatever may hold true of God's 'Word' as having the character of revelation, and whatever may hold true of promise and faith — these concepts are and remain empty categories if, so far as content is concerned, they are not saturated with references to Christ." [5] This calls to mind the many eloquent songs of praise to God for "the preservation of His Word in all its truth and purity" with little and less than eloquent reference to the truth as it is revealed in the incarnation, life, suffering, crucifixion, death, and resurrection of Christ, with little or no sharing of Him who has purified us in Baptism and cleansed us with His blood in the Holy Supper. It is amazing how much theology, not only of the speculative variety that takes place in mythical ivory towers, but that which is preached day in and day out on the grass roots level, fails to be "saturated with references to Christ." One might pardon non-Gospel theology in the ivory tower. One might, I say, for supposedly ivory towers have few listeners. On the grass roots level non-Gospel theology approaches the unpardonable.

"For I am not ashamed of the Gospel; it is the power of God for salvation to everyone who has faith . . ." (Rom. 1:16). If the Gospel is the power of God for salvation, then nothing else is power for that purpose. Not to speak the Gospel is to be powerless in that moment when power is most needed. If the Gospel is the power, the avoidance of the use of power is hard to explain and harder to pardon. Commissions, committees, study groups designed to study the church's problems would do well to look at this land of presupposition, the land of Gospel proclamation, and ask simply, "Is the Gospel being proclaimed as we suppose it is?"

Perhaps the memory of the catacombs and of Nero's torches and lions is too much with us. The Neronian image is the dominant picture we have of a man ready to confess the Gospel without shame . . . with lions and flames taking alternate turns licking his feet. The rarity with which the Gospel is spoken without the stimulus-threat

5 Werner Elert, *The Structure of Lutheranism*, trans. Walter A. Hansen (St. Louis: Concordia Publishing Hosue, 1962), p. 66.

value of flames or lions would lead us to believe either that the Gospel is something we have to be ashamed of or that it is not the power of God, or a bit of both. The volcanic eruption of the Gospel throughout the New Testament under all kinds of circumstances would indicate the permissibility of speaking the Gospel in our own time under more than "backs against the wall, machine gun in the face" conditions.

THE ANSWER TO NON-GOSPEL

The preceding paragraphs make two observations: (1) to a frightening degree the Gospel is not spoken, (2) preachers preaching non-Gospel would be horrified to learn they had been doing just that.

What then must be said to say the Gospel?

Christ Himself once put it this way: "'These are My words which I spoke to you, while I was still with you, that everything written about Me in the law of Moses and the prophets and the psalms must be fulfilled.' Then He opened their minds to understand the Scriptures, and said to them, 'Thus it is written, that the Christ should suffer and on the third day rise from the dead, and that repentance and forgiveness of sins should be preached in His name to all nations, beginning from Jerusalem. You are witnesses of these things'" (Luke 24:44-48). That is the way Christ once answered the question, "What must be said to say Gospel?" According to Him if repentance and remission of sins are to continue, their proclamation must crackle with His suffering, death, and resurrection. This, incidentally or not so incidentally, is the key to opening up the Scriptures.

Dr. Caemmerer's description of the Gospel content of preaching includes

> 1. Jesus of Nazareth, born in Bethlehem, a teacher in Galilee and Judea, crucified in Jerusalem, is the Messiah planned by God to redeem His people.
>
> 2. According to that same plan, announced in the Old Testament Scriptures, He rose from the dead and thus still lives and rules.
>
> 3. The story of His life, death, and resurrection is a message which His followers proclaim to their world and to each other.
>
> 4. This message has turning and changing power, bringing the thrust of God's own life to bear on those who hear it.

5. It has this power because it conveys the forgiveness of sins,
which is the purpose of Christ's death and resurrection.

Two other ingredients were explicitly in the message already
in the days of the apostles: this Christ is at once the man Jesus and
the Son of the living God; and He will return in glory to reign
forever.[6]

At the conclusion of an exhaustive study of this same question,
The Basic Content of the Christian Gospel, the author wrote, "In
summary, then, we might affirm that to enunciate the basic content
of the Gospel one must state that it is God's doing from beginning
to end, that this plan of God took form in a very specific Person who
died (one of His titles is Jesus of Nazareth), that this Person rose
again from the dead, and without fail it must be said that repentance
and forgiveness of sins are now being offered by and through this
Person and/or act."[7] The attempt in this study was to arrive at an
irreducible minimum of content which would still guarantee Gospel
proclamation. Even with that as the objective — an objective one
would not want to pursue normally in preaching: making sure one
had only minimum Gospel — the irreducible still insists on stating
that Christ's action originated in God, that Christ carried out that
action by His death and resurrection, that the proclamation of this
action is now the power through which the life of God goes to work
in the life of man. Nothing of the peripheral or the ephemeral in
these four items, just hard-core content. That is what makes their
absence in preaching so hard to excuse.

Luther's explanation of the Second Article of the Apostles' Creed,
often praised for the precision and completeness of its statement on
the atonement, just as often ignored as a guideline and inspiration
with which to measure the precision and completeness of the statement of the atonement in preaching, is still just that — one of the
best ways of determining whether our preaching is only religious
word-making or if it is Gospel proclamation.

"The 'rule' of the pastor consists in this, that he *serves* the sinner
with the Word of promise, with the forgiveness of sins. Therefore
Christ established the office because, as He who was crucified and
was raised from the dead, He wanted to bestow forgiveness, and

6   Richard R. Caemmerer, *Preaching for the Church* (St. Louis: Concordia
Publishing House, 1959), pp. 5—6.

7   Paul W. F. Harms, *The Basic Content of the Christian Gospel* (Unpublished Master's Thesis: Concordia Seminary, St. Louis, 1954), p. 54.

because after His exaltation it is necessary for others to proclaim the fact that He bestows forgiveness." [8]

Dr. Caemmerer describes a common factor which often deceives the preacher into believing he has preached the Gospel when in fact he has not. "First and last the preacher must face the fact that he not merely describes goals but leads to them; that he not merely describes repentance or summons to repentance but is God's agent for working it. Entire traditions of religious thought and preaching assume that when the preacher has described what God wants and has urged to it, the preacher is through. But then his work has just begun. He must still speak the Word of life. He must still convey the power from God that moves the hearer in God's direction." [9] This is probably one of the most deceptive, elusive, clever Gospel substitutes — diagnosis of a problem, prescription of the new direction. It deceives the experienced preacher no less than the neophyte. Both diagnosis and prescription are necessary, both are helpful. Both alone mislead the preacher and his listener, for they can be convinced that the preacher has done his task, and all the while the one thing needful is missing, the Word of life.

"By making an offer the Gospel becomes a promise. It does not want to instruct; it wants to bestow a gift. It does not want to convict the knowledge of sin of being in error; it wants to convey forgiveness of sin." [10] "His aim is to make you partake of a kind of experience that he has had, rather than to make you accept some dogmatic belief," wrote T. S. Eliot of the writings of Charles Williams.[11] That is also a way of expressing the intention of preaching. Preaching is done to have us share in the forgiveness of sins, in the suffering, the crucifixion, the death, the resurrection, the ascension of Christ. Diagnosis, goal-direction, proclaiming of judgment in the Law — all is done so that the Word of life might be held high for all eyes to see.

As Christ approached the very moment of the crucifixion, He asked, "What shall I say? 'Father, save Me from this hour'?" He answered His own question dramatically: "No, for this purpose I have

8 Elert, p. 345.

9 Caemmerer, *Preaching for the Church*, p. 19.

10 Elert, pp. 65—66.

11 Charles Williams, *All Hallows' Eve* (New York: The Noonday Press), p. xiv.

come to this hour" (John 12:27). Our objective is not to avoid the cross any more than it was Christ's objective. If He felt that the crucifixion was the cause for which He had come to this hour, then *speaking* the crucifixion must be the cause for which we have come to this hour.

The question is not infrequent, "Must the preacher speak the atonement in every sermon?" Christ answers this question as well as anyone when He tells His disciples that He "must go unto Jerusalem and suffer many things . . . and be killed and be raised again the third day." "Be it far from Thee, Lord," answered Peter. To which Christ gave the cutting reply, "Get thee behind Me, Satan . . . thou savorest not the things . . . of God." This is a good answer for us when we raise the question, "Must I speak the atonement in my preaching on every occasion?" A subtle, satanic carelessness if not a satanic motivation stands behind our avoidance of the atonement.

The New Testament speaks Gospel language often and in full regalia. One need only quote some opening phrases to recall that fullness: "The Word was made flesh and dwelt among us . . ." "When the fullness of the time was come . . ." "God was in Christ reconciling the world unto Himself . . ." "Do you not know that all of us who have been baptized into Christ Jesus were baptized into His death?" The sermons in Acts 2, 3, 4, 5, 10, and 13 are useful in awakening a sluggish memory. Interpenetration of Gospel in most of the epistles is helpful in showing us how Gospel preaching is to be done.

Two statements from our Lord Himself serve as a directive for the preacher if he would be a preacher of the Gospel. "And as Moses lifted up the serpent in the wilderness, so must the Son of Man be lifted up, that whoever believes in Him may have eternal life" (John 3:14-15). "And I, when I am lifted up from the earth, will draw all men to Myself" (John 12:32). If preaching does not lift Christ up for all to see, lift Him up via Word, voice, and gesture as He was originally held high by the cross, then preaching is not preaching, at least not preaching the Gospel.

Few of us preachers are such consummate artists with words that we can with no mention of Christ by name, no reference to His becoming flesh, no mention of His suffering, no reference to His crucifixion, no reference to His resurrection or ascension create in the minds of hearers the picture of God's definitive action in Christ Jesus from incarnation, through life, suffering, crucifixion, death, resurrection, to ascension. In fact, most of us have a difficult time getting people to think of Christ as Lord, as Savior, as Redeemer, through direct referral to His name and to His action. We seldom think about what we are not asked to think about, especially in group situations. There are hindrances enough to thinking about what we are asked to think about. Sometimes that can be our salvation — shutting our minds to the vivid call of advertisements in the midst of a television presentation of Shakespeare's *Hamlet*. Sometimes it can well lead to our judgment — in the midst of preaching when we are led to (or let ourselves) think about anything else except what God wants us to think about, the person of His Son Jesus Christ.

A One-Topic Power Ministry

Perhaps the question of the necessity of speaking the Gospel whenever preaching takes place would be obviated if we realized that preaching must not so much contain Gospel as *be* Gospel. If a sermon must only contain Gospel, then the Gospel soon gets the status of being just one topic among many. The question gets a surer answer if we rephrase it this way, "Must every sermon proclaim God as He has revealed Himself in Jesus Christ?" "What else?" comes the answer. To preach the Gospel is to preach Jesus Christ as God's servant for our sake to our need: ". . . that Christ may dwell in your hearts through faith; that you, being rooted and grounded in love, may have power to comprehend with all the saints what is the breadth and length and height and depth and to know the love of Christ which surpasses knowledge, that you may be filled with all the fullness of God" (Eph. 3:17-19). To be filled with all the fullness of God takes all of the fullness of God. The Gospel has the fullness of God. God wishes to fill us with all the fullness of Himself. He can hardly do that with a dash of Gospel here and there. The proclamation of Himself, therefore, must not only contain Gospel, it must be Gospel.

To put it another way. The Gospel is not one topic among many open to the Christian preacher to choose or reject as he may. It is *the* topic, not the chief of topics, but the topic, the only topic. This is what Paul means in stating that he was determined not to know anything except Jesus Christ and Him crucified. He says this not to restrict the potential topics he might have as a speaker. He was determined not to know anything but Jesus Christ and Him crucified, because that topic comprised and covered all others. "For He has made known to us in all wisdom and insight the mystery of His will, according to His purpose which He set forth in Christ as a plan for the fullness of time, to unite all things in Him, things in heaven and things on earth" (Eph. 1:9-10). "To unite all things in Him, things in heaven and things on earth" — that was the objective of Christ's coming. That is the objective of preaching. Paul repeats himself in Col. 1:19: "For in Him all the fullness of God was pleased to dwell, and through Him to reconcile to Himself all things, whether on earth or in heaven, making peace by the blood of His cross." The Gospel, just as the Christ of the Gospel, is that power which creates the new unity. If that objective took the full measure of God's action in Jesus Christ from Incarnation to Ascension, then it takes the full measure of the Gospel now to achieve that same objective. The Gospel is Christ in action now.

Just as the Gospel covers the totality of all that is in heaven and in earth, so it covers the totality of all that is in a man. "To them God chose to make known how great among the Gentiles are the riches of the glory of this mystery, which is Christ in you, the hope of glory. Him we proclaim, warning every man and teaching every man in all wisdom, that we may present every man mature in Christ. For this I toil, striving with all the energy which He mightily inspires within me" (Col. 1:27-29). If maturity in Christ is the objective for every man, it takes the fullness and the maturity of Christ to achieve that. A man becomes mature in Christ through Christ, the Christ whom St. Paul then and the preacher now strive with all energy to inspire within every man. Notice again how the Gospel is not one power among many through which a man becomes mature in Christ, but the only power. It has total coverage.

"He [the preacher] has to brace himself to move his hearers with but one lever resting on one fulcrum — the power of the Spirit employing the fact and reminder of the redeeming work of Jesus Christ . . . for he wants action, not any kind of action at any price or for any cause but only that action which God Himself produces." [12] "Therefore, if anyone is in Christ, he is a new creation; the old has passed away, behold, the new has come. All this is from God, who through Christ reconciled us to Himself and gave us the ministry

12   Caemmerer, *Preaching for the Church,* p. 38.

of reconciliation; that is, God was in Christ reconciling the world to Himself, not counting their trespasses against them, and entrusting to us the message of reconciliation. So we are ambassadors for Christ, God making His appeal through us. We beseech you on behalf of Christ, be reconciled to God. For our sake He made Him to be sin who knew no sin, so that in Him we might become the righteousness of God" (2 Cor. 5:17-21). In this brief passage we get a picture of God's re-creative power in action. The means with which He did His re-creation, making all things new, and the means through which the re-creation is continued, note well, are the same. Christ did it through Word and action. Preaching does it now through communication of that action.

"We cannot but speak of what we have seen and heard" (Acts 4:20). A beautiful woman, newly engaged, may finally tire of displaying and praising her engagement ring. We dare never tire of speaking of the things we have seen and heard. What are the things we have seen and heard? Once more, it is Christ at the request of the Father interrupting life in our sphere as a full participant in that life, which includes a crucifixion and a death but also a resurrection and an ascension. And the "must speak" is hardly the "must" of duty but the "must" of joy which can never take crucifixions and resurrections in comfortable, taken-for-granted stride.

A look at the epistles of Paul soon convinces us that he has but one topic — God, atonement, Christ — from His incarnation to His ascension. For him the Gospel is not one of many topics in a list compounded of incest, stewardship, evangelism, husband and wife relationships, church-state relations, responsibility for the poor. It is always Gospel, Gospel in relation to — but Gospel. It interpenetrates whatever he says. It would not be an accurate appraisal to say that what he says always contains the Gospel. It is the Gospel.

"My little children, with whom I am again in travail until Christ be formed in you!" (Gal. 4:19). Perhaps if the object of a preacher's travail were more often "the formation of Christ" in the hearers, both he and his listeners would bear the travail more readily. For it would be travail with a purpose and direction, a clear direction, the formation of Christ. Just having that clear goal in mind on every occasion, the preacher would find strength, courage, joy that he has never known. It is the being in travail "for we know not what" that is exhausting. Even the most splendid budget or the most brilliant evangelism program (especially one without the evangel) do not quite match the fullness that is to be found in Christ. One can plunge fully into Him without fear of exhausting Him. One can be in travail a good long time if one knows he is giving birth to Christ in another human being and not an abortion. It is a travail which is more than endured. It is enjoyed for the very joy that is set before us. The preaching must thus *be* Gospel not only for the sake of the hearer but for the sake of the preacher. In his very preaching the Holy Spirit is trying to form Christ in the preacher as well as in the church.

Preaching, that it might do what it recommends, must be *kerygma.* It must needs be Gospel. It must liberate, give sight to the blind, not just suggest that seeing is superior to blindness. It must give hearing to the deaf, not just recommend that hearing is better than deafness. It must straighten the legs of the cripple, not just recommend that walking is better than crawling. It must rid the body of leprosy, not just recommend that health is better than illness. No matter how glowing the picture of health, there will not be much health given unless the Great Physician is in attendance. The Gospel must equip. There is only One who does that. When He is absent, do not be surprised that no equipping, no healing, no freeing, no encouraging, no strengthening goes on. He does all of these. And if He is to do them, He must be present. If all things in heaven and in earth are to be united in Him and if all things within a man are to be united in Him, we can hardly expect Him to do His work by absenting Himself. A snippet of Gospel talk at irregular intervals can hardly serve adequately for Him to fill all in all in the universe, for Him to mature the individual into the fullness of God Himself.

Yet No Magic Formula

To speak the Gospel is to do more, however, than parrot a formula of words which smacks of atonement vocabulary. How often a topic on stewardship, marriage, war on communism is suddenly interrupted by a preacher's jamming in a paragraph damning the meritoriousness of good works and praising justification by faith (true enough in their own way but in a way utterly unrelated to what had been occupying his mind and the minds of the audience just a moment before). It is not that Christ or His incarnation or His resurrection or His atoning work has nothing to say to the issues of marriage or communism or stewardship. Quite the opposite. But

to speak Atonement vocabulary in an unrelated way is not a conveying of the Atonement and the power for salvation. No Gospel formula in the last paragraph on page 8 of a manuscript can rectify all
the bad theology of the first seven pages, nor can it be cited as proof
of Gospel preaching. For the Gospel must not only be there, it must
be there in full relationship to the issues of the moment.

Not only must Gospel words be spoken, but also the thoughts,
the ideas must be in the words in such a way that they turn out
to be Gospel — the difference between the dry bones of Ezekiel
before and after they began breathing the breath of life. French
Gospel words may be Gospel for the ears of a Frenchman. They will
hardly be Gospel for the ears of a Russian. No group of words carries a magical guarantee to produce unfailingly in the mind and
heart of the hearer the triumphant Christ ready to share His triumph
with all — not even the words of John 3:16. On a given occasion
spoken by a given preacher, John 3:16 may be the signal for 20 min-
utes of uninterrupted boredom.

THE WORD AND WORDS

Not only must Gospel be spoken to be Gospel, it must be spoken
to the moment, to the issue. The best cue for this comes from our
Lord's incarnation. To redeem man, He became man, not a sheep
or a goat, or even an angel, but man. He "became flesh and dwelt
among us." In the same way the Gospel, which is God in action
in the flesh now among men as Christ was once in action in the flesh,
must be made incarnate.

If we are talking sheep language, we had better talk shepherd
language to go with it; if we are talking night language, we had
better talk day language; with slavery language, the language of
freedom; with orphan language, the language of adoption; with lost
language, the language of found; with death language, the language
of life; with hostility language, the language of reconciliation.[13] That
is, to speak the Gospel to the moment, the choice of Gospel language
and imagery must seek to make the Gospel incarnate for that moment
to that situation. Accurate doctrinal formulations of the Gospel, even
the standard formulation of justification, may fail to bring the

13   Ps. 23, Luke 15, Gal. 4—5; 2 Cor. 5. See also Joseph Sittler, *The Ecology
of Faith* (Philadelphia: Muhlenberg [Fortress] Press, 1961); Helmut Thielicke,
How the World Began, trans. John W. Doberstein (Philadelphia: Muhlenberg
Press, 1961), esp. ch. 20.

Gospel to bear because its imagery may have little to do with the imagery of the need diagnosed.

The nakedness of Adam is met with the nakedness of Christ on the cross, not by justification by faith. The rebellious sonship of an Absalom is met with the faithful sonship of Christ in His crucifixion, not by justification by faith. The melancholy of the preacher in Ecclesiastes is met by our Lord who for the joy that was set before Him endured the cross despising the shame, not by justification by faith. To shift suddenly and resolutely and inflexibly to justification by faith when justification by any other means is not the topic is as much out of place — if the preacher is concerned about communicating the Gospel — as if he were at the crucial moment in a conversation to switch to French for a hearer who understood only Swahili. The preacher who made a radical language switch like this would readily understand why he would not be understood. Even if the words remain technically all English, the need to avoid this changeover to a different language in the communication of the Gospel is no less a concern. Words can all be from the English language for English people and still communicate nothing but chaff or obscurity, all in the guise of communicating the Gospel.

No Room for Don Quixote Pulpiteers

Not only must the language of the Gospel "fit in" with the language of analysis and diagnosis to be Gospel. The problems analyzed must be of genuine concern for the listener. The Gospel can be of little help in bringing the power of salvation to bear if it is bringing its power to bear on nonexisting problems. This is not a matter of Gospel adequacy but of diagnostic adequacy. Do the syndromes diagnosed from the pulpit turn out in fact to be the ones which actually are a pain for people, or for that matter, even for the preacher himself? Often I have felt uneasy about the great gulf fixed between the pre- and/or post-worship sacristy talk. And I must confess that the pre- and/or post-talk often seem closer to reality than the chancel conversation. Perhaps a close comparison of problems diagnosed in our preaching content over the past years and those daily highlighted in newspapers, books, magazines, plays, works of art, would be revealing. The criticism often heard about the unreality of preaching, the lack of correlation between preaching and bearing the burden and heat of the day is not easy to bear, but unfortunately too much of it is accurate.

Preaching the Gospel in its fullness, but preaching it to irrelevant concerns, is not preaching the Gospel. Unless it meets people where they are just as Christ met people where they were in His days in the flesh, we will of necessity become more and more the magician attributing hocus-pocus qualities to "Thy Word will not return unto Me void," even though we preach it from a void to a void.

THE ROAD TO ILLUSION

If among all his doubts the preacher never doubts that the Gospel of Jesus Christ is the power of God unto salvation, what keeps him from using that power unremittingly and to the full? Once having decided that oxygen and eating are essential to living, rare is that man who succeeds for long in abandoning either oxygen or food or both. Why then? For one thing, there are the presuppositions already referred to, false presuppositions, but presuppositions, nevertheless: (a) if one knows the fact of Christ, one need not speak it, (b) to speak it would be to speak the obvious and so lose the attention of the audience concerned about other matters, (c) the listener will automatically supply the Gospel even when not spoken, (d) the Gospel may be necessary at all times when speaking to the non-Christian, but the level of necessity drops sharply for those who are Christians, (e) it is enough if preaching *have* some Gospel vocabulary; it need not *be* Gospel.

Secondly, a necessary and justified concern with diagnosis of ailment and prescription for cure is often substituted for a preaching of the Gospel. This is a danger not only for the careless preacher but especially for the one who cares. His concern to see change in the listeners can make him concentrate so strongly on the direction for change that he forgets the power for change. The very brilliance of his diagnosis and the warmth of conviction for the direction of change can mislead both himself and his listeners to believe that the Gospel, the very power for change, has been provided. Yet a careful check reveals only diagnosis and prescription, no Gospel. In effect, this approach lets deaf people know that they are deaf, informs them of the wonder and the joy they can have in hearing, but fails to provide the hearing aid or the necessary surgery to make hearing possible. The deaf person may rejoice to learn that his problem is not blindness.

If the prescription artist is also vividly descriptive about the joys of hearing, he may beguile the deaf man into a momentary, imaginary pleasure of hearing. The hard fact of the matter is, however, he is still deaf.

A CHOICE IN FOOLISHNESSES

Thirdly, we do not speak the Gospel or at least do not do it very effectively because of a misleading phrase in the Scripture itself, ". . . it pleased God by the foolishness of preaching to save them that believe" (1 Cor. 1:21 ff.). "Preaching" here is taken in its popular context, largely the act of making religious words from behind a stone, wooden, steel, or concrete barrier. It is this word-making process which is thought of as foolishness. If God had wanted the Gospel proclaimed through some other process — titanium manufacturing, balloon launchings, waterfall diversions, this conceivably would not be foolishness. It is that God chooses the word-making processes for Gospel sharing that deserves the description: foolishness.

If that interpretation is correct, several comfortable consequences result. If the Bible calls preaching foolishness, it would be vanity on my part to try to make it make sense. In fact, there is nothing I can do to make it make sense. In fact, I had better do nothing to make it make sense. Out of this kind of thinking grows a heresy: parallel to the doctrine that the Holy Spirit does it all, despite the foolishness of preaching, is the doctrine that my careless preaching not only carries with it a perpetual absolution, there is actually no need even for my confession. Carelessness in preaching thus carries with it a divine blessing. Who are we to lessen the foolishness of God by introducing order where God ordered chaos?

There is only one problem with this thesis: The Greek will not allow it. Word making is no more foolish than water washing and bread baking. The foolishness is here identified with the *kerygma,* the atonement. God's action of invading the world with Christ's action . . . this is what is designated foolishness, not the word-making about it. Foolishness refers to the content and the intent of the message proclaimed — the proclamation. To put it more accurately, "It pleased God through the foolishness of Christ's birth, life, suffering, crucifixion, and resurrection to save them that believed." Preaching, in this instance, is the same as Christ Jesus as Lord.

Consequently, because of a basic misinterpretation, preaching — the pulpit kind — often does not rise to God's kind of foolishness. One cannot be foolish in God's way unless one speaks the Gospel. Preaching, the misinterpreted kind, rises or falls with the preacher's foolishness. God's kind never has a chance. The foolishness of "the proclamation of Christ as Lord" must be kept separate from any kind of foolishness we may introduce by our carelessness, poor preparation, or just plain failure in a given instance to see that Christ is formed in the listener by sharing the power of the resurrection with him.

Almost, but Not Quite, Until

If the assertions up to this point have brought joy by their reemphasis on the centrality of the Gospel in Christian preaching — and that the Gospel alone is the true proclamation, and without it we have no preaching in the New Testament sense — let that joy be held in abeyance until we have crossed one more hurdle. The Gospel, we have said, is the power of God unto salvation, not the *assertion* that the Gospel is the power of God. Agreement that the Gospel, and not something else, is the power of God unto salvation is not the same as speaking it in a given moment. The fact that I have the Gospel in the back of my mind is not the same as having it in the front of my mind, is not the same as speaking what is in the front of my mind to the ears and heart of the listener.

All of our talk of doctrinal virginity suffers prostitution if on a given Sunday morning at 10:30 the Gospel does not get spoken, if at a sickbed on a given Thursday night the Gospel does not get spoken, if the "pulpit," whatever that may be at a given moment, does not serve as the launching pad for the Gospel.

The hearer will not very readily be thinking about what the preacher is not talking about in that moment. In fact, he may not even be thinking about what the preacher *is* saying. This is as true of the Gospel as of anything else. The Ford salesman concentrates on getting his customer to think about Fords by talking about Fords, not about onions or lemons. The mathematics teacher gets the student to concentrate on two-plus-two by talking about addition. The Greek professor gets his student to concentrate on the optative by discussing the optative, not the gerundive. Even the "soft sell" artist makes sure that the customer thinks about the product that provides the salesman with his income. What is true in these very elementary matters is even more true in the speaking of the Gospel. If God's redemptive work and that alone is the power, that is what the listener must be compelled to think about. The preacher tells the listener to think Gospel as he speaks Gospel. In other words, the preacher should not be surprised if the listener does not think atonement, *kerygma,* incarnation, crucifixion, death, resurrection when he (the preacher) does not think about it or speak about it himself. In fact, in time the preacher should get accustomed to the listeners' not thinking atonement even if he *has* been talking it, successful communication being the difficult thing that it is.

It is not enough for the church to believe the Gospel to be the power of God unto salvation, not enough for it to assert that it is the power. The church must speak it so that its power can be released. It must speak it in the given moment and the given occasion to the given need. We can no more assume that the Gospel can do its work without our speaking it than we can assume that oxygen will do its work without our breathing it, all theories about the excellencies of either or both to the contrary. For a given moment of word-making to be preaching, New Testament style, means that moment must be word-making about Christ's victorious action from His birth to His ascension.

The church's task is not to possess the Gospel but to speak it. When the preacher has safely passed this hurdle of actually speaking the Gospel on a given occasion in a given moment to a given need, then there is time for joy; for only then, but then indeed, can he count himself a preacher of the Gospel.

CHAPTER BIBLIOGRAPHY

Backus, William. *An Analysis of Missouri Synod Sermons Based on the Content of the New Testament Kerygma* (unpublished master's thesis), St. Louis: Concordia Seminary, 1952.

Caemmerer, Richard R. *The Church in the World.* St. Louis: Concordia Publishing House, 1949.

————. "The Gospel to Be Preached," *A Symposium of Essays and Addresses Given at the Counselors Conference,* The Lutheran Church — Missouri Synod, Valparaiso, Ind. (Sept. 1960), pp. 82—91.

————. *Preaching for the Church.* St. Louis: Concordia Publishing House,

Elert, Werner. 1959. *The Structure of Lutheranism,* trans. Walter A. Hansen: St. Louis: Concordia Publishing House, 1962.

Harms, Paul W. F. *The Basic Content of the Christian Gospel* (unpublished master's thesis). St. Louis: Concordia Seminary, 1954.

Sittler, Joseph. *The Ecology of Faith.* Philadelphia: Muhlenberg [Fortress] Press, 1961.

Thielicke, Helmut. *How the World Began,* trans. John W. Doberstein. 2d print. Philadelphia: Muhlenberg [Fortress] Press, 1961.

William, Charles. *All Hallows' Eve.* New York: The Noonday Press.

"... the worship of the church as the action of God's people simultaneously up to God in adoration, sidewise to one another in the word of edification."

CHAPTER 5

The Church at Worship

KENNETH F. KORBY

Life is worship. The real issue in worship is set between idolatry, which is death, and faith, which is participation in the life of God. Reality gives man no third way, for God has so created and established man that he can never cease being a creature whose beginning and end are firmly tied to earth. From dust he is taken; to dust he returns. In between his beginning and end God is always near, both supporting his life and at the same time taking his life away because he is a sinner. Man's worship is his passionate quest for understanding his beginning so that he may control his end. Man's worship, his idolatry, is the ceaseless activity to save his life from the death that overshadows him in his most fundamental and inescapable boundness to the earth — in food and drink, in clothing and life. Those points at which death manifests itself (sex, food, work, fame, meaning) are the points at which man is captivated by the fascination to look for and expect the breakthrough to real life. Worship is man's attempt to find life and to break death, or at least to overcome it. Life is worship. "No one can serve two masters; for either he will hate the one and love the other, or he will be devoted to the one and despise the other. You cannot serve God and mammon." [1]

[1] Matt. 6:24. All Bible references, unless otherwise indicated, are to the Revised Standard Version. On the conflict between faith in true worship and in idolatry, see the classic study by Vilmos Vajta, *Die Theologie des Gottesdienstes bei Luther,* 3d ed., Forschungen Zur Kirchen- und Dogmengeschichte, No. 1 (Göttingen: Vandenhoeck & Ruprecht, 1959), pp. 3 ff. A somewhat shortened version of Vajta's work is available in English, *An Interpretation: Luther on Worship,* trans.

It does not follow that worship is life. Idolatry is death, both now and forever. False gods devour their devotees. Men who seek their lives in food and drink, in work and play, in religion or irreligion are consumed by the gods they make and by the "liturgy of anxiety" they offer to those gods. They lose, but never find, their lives. This is not to say that idolaters have no dealings with God. He indeed deals with them, sustaining their lives in a particular relationship to Himself. In fact, it is God's presence and activity which threaten men in these very points of contact with their lives. Anxiety in men is not groundless. Men cannot control their lives, yet they do not trust God for their lives. Anxiety is the liturgy of their idolatry.[2]

Worship is life when it is the worship of the true God, for the true God is living and He gives life to those who trust His Gospel for righteousness. God seeks men to worship Him. He wills that His life be lived in men. This is the nature of divine love, that it draws to itself those with whom it desires to share its own life. God seeks men to worship Him in spirit and in truth. Such people are the true worshipers. "God is spirit, and those who worship Him must worship in spirit and truth" (John 4:24). It follows that there are false worshipers, and to them Jesus bluntly says: "You worship what you do not know." (John 4:22)

False worship is false not because people do not have the Bible (the Samaritans had and accepted at least the Books of Moses), nor because men worship in a specific locality with specific forms, using materials of the created world. To define "spiritual worship" as "inward" and "nonmaterial," done best without externals, is to be deceived by a too-widespread heresy.[3] Nor is the idolatry merely an absolutizing of the relative (although that is present). What is false about false worship is that man, having his life threatened in and

Ulrich S. Leupold (Philadelphia: Muhlenberg [Fortress] Press, 1958), pp. 3 ff. Above all, see Luther's own comments in his exposition of the First Commandment in the Large Catechism in *The Book of Concord: The Confessions of the Evangelical Lutheran Church,* trans. and ed. Theodore G. Tappert in collaboration with Jaroslav Pelikan, Robert H. Fischer, and Arthur C. Piepkorn (Philadelphia: Muhlenberg [Fortress] Press, 1959), pp. 365—71. (Hereafter this work is cited as Tappert.)

2 See Jesus' words (Matt. 6:25-30) and the conclusion of His diagnosis: "O men of little faith."

3 See Luther's discussion of this erroneous notion of "spiritual" in his *Confession Concerning Christ's Supper,* in *Luther's Works,* trans. and ed. Robert H. Fischer (Philadelphia: Muhlenberg [Fortress] Press, 1961), 37, 235—52. There are some helpful arguments on the John 4 passage in George S. Hendry, *The Christian Doctrine of the Holy Spirit* (Philadelphia: Westminster Press, 1956), pp. 31 ff.

through the created world, turns to the creations of his mind and spirit, to the religion of his heart and to the sensual objects of creation, first to conceal his life from God and then to save his life from God. This is his idolatry, his blindness. In whatever way he defines what he seeks, he is driven by the hope and confidence that he will find life in the things he uses, in the actions he does, and in the thoughts he thinks. In the matter of the created world, or in the creations of his mind, he looks for what makes his life right, permanent, and meaningful.

God's search for man to worship Him in spirit and in truth always begins with God calling man back to Himself, placing him before His scrutiny and gaze. God visits man, He looks at him. That man is addressed who has been deceived to death, who knows shame and lostness, who, being fearful of exposure, creates phony garments to hide himself from his fellows and from God. God's voice and Word are working in the created world.[4] Within the very structures of life where man hides himself, God's Word calls him to account. God Himself addresses him with the question, "Where are you?" Although man cannot escape the structures of created life, God's activity in them on man and through him are not unambiguously clear to man. God's sovereign providence gives and sustains life for man, but that life is also overshadowed by death. With death life itself is defeated. Hence man experiences shame and anxiety while he is sustained in a plenitude of gifts. He is cramped and lost where he cannot escape.

However, it is God's address to man which reveals his real situation. God's Word calling man to account does not create the lostness but manifests it. God's Word increases the dread lostness. Furthermore, God cuts through the lies, deceit, and self-excuse which are the ongoing inner dialog of the sinner. In the Gen. 3 account man is stripped of his fig leaves. God's Word plunges him into the truth about himself, for God reveals his mistrust of God and its resulting disobedience. Death no longer works as a silent shadow over man's life; God's address to him has thrown light on it, that God may be glorified and every mouth stopped.

God's intention is not to leave man naked and dead, but to reclothe him and send him out into the world. The word of promise

---

[4] Gen. 3:8: "And they heard the sound of the Lord God walking in the garden in the cool of the day, and the man and his wife hid themselves from the presence of God among the trees of the garden."

is preached to him. This word of promise overcomes the word of death; it overcomes death itself. It is the expression of God's will that man live — and that he live in hope. Hence, man's life is reclothed. God does not destroy the created structures by the promise; He plunges renewed man back into those relationships, with glory itself resting upon him who is called.

No clearer illustration of this work of God the Caller and Purifier of the existence of those who are called can be given than that of Isaiah. Distressed by the unexpected and shattering death of Uzziah, Isaiah is in the temple worshiping God (Is. 6). Confronted by the glorious sovereignty of God, Isaiah is terror-stricken because he is a sinner. God's activity in worship is to cleanse Isaiah by purification. Through a designated messenger the lips of Isaiah are burned clean and he, willingly joining the work of God, becomes one sent to speak the Word of God to the people.

The church at worship is moved by God's speaking action, for by calling men before Himself and judging them, God reveals the true character of their life as sinners. By His Word God plunges the called into the truth about themselves. In worship they break through to that truth. By God's Word their idolatry is revealed, judged, and destroyed. In worship the church gives glory to God in the first place by being confessed sinners in truth. And yet, precisely God's glory is that by calling shameful men to Himself He redresses them in a life of hope. He purifies them by cutting them loose from death and reestablishing them in life.

Stripping away deception and re-creating men in truth is truly God's work in worship because of and in Jesus Christ's death and resurrection, His ascension and intercession, His pouring out of the Spirit and His promise to return. Jesus Christ in His life and ministry is the paradigm of the church at worship. Both the judgment of God putting death to death, and the promise of life — given as a favor — are done fully in Jesus Christ. He is the only-begotten of the Father, the Word full of grace and truth, born of the Virgin Mary, born into the world of time and place, whom God Himself called by the name "Jesus." He is called Jesus because He saves His people from their sins. This is the name by which God calls men to Himself. His is also the name by which those who are called call upon God in true worship.

Jesus Christ is the first and true worshiper in spirit and in truth.

He is the Head of the church, the Leader of the called. In Him all worship is in spirit and truth, for He is the God-ordained man to fulfill the Law on our behalf by dying the death without in any way mistrusting that God would raise Him from the dead. Jesus Christ perfects all worship in that He gives His life for the world. His worship is true, for He entrusted Himself to God, even in the death resulting from God's curse. He offered Himself to God in the spirit, and through Him God conquered death for men. God thereby does His full work of holy love: He overthrows the kingdom of sin and death, and raises up new life that never dies. He gives the Spirit that this life in man may be full and free. Jesus' altar for offering His self-oblation is the cross. His life is the sacrifice He offers, in which offering He is also the Priest. It follows from this that the shape and content of the church's worship is union with Jesus Christ in His death and resurrection, effected by the Spirit through the High Priest's continuing intercession for the church.

God calls men into this work of Christ by the proclamation issuing out of the mouth of His people. The living Lord shares Himself in the plenitude of His grace and gifts through His distribution of the Lord's Supper and through Baptism in His name, which things are done through human hands. Where and when the Spirit wills, He works these works. The heart of all worship by the church is to receive this Christ with His benefits.[5] The response which seizes upon the quickening forgiveness of sins given by God in the spoken story of Christ for us is the celebration of the triumph of God in Christ.[6] God is most exquisitely glorified as God precisely as the church at worship abandons her own life, sinks her own sins into Christ's death and burial, and celebrates in Christ's resurrection the sure fact of her own new life.

Such transaction in worship is not effected in view of the fact that the church at worship uses words and actions. Rather, God calls the church by the Gospel — by the words and actions about Christ for us — to take a share in Christ's death and life and, taking a share,

[5] Cf. Ap IV (Tappert, p. 114).

[6] Cf. Luther's comments of faith as decisive in receiving the revelation, in his comments on Ps. 90, *Luther's Works,* ed. Jaroslav Pelikan (St. Louis: Concordia Publishing House, 1956), 13, 88. For a splendid essay on worship as response see Christhard Mahrenhold, "Das Wesen des christlichen Gottesdienstes," *Musicologica et Liturgica,* herausgegeben von Karl Ferdinand Muller (Kassel: Bärenreiter, 1960), pp. 284—95.

to be united with Him.[7] When the church at worship confesses her sin, she is emboldened to enter into God's judgment, not by the self-righteous notion that having gone through the proper steps she will arrive at forgiveness for rescue, but by the reality of the forgiveness in Christ which re-creates the church by means of the words spoken in her worship and the actions that are congruent with those words. In the words of the Easter Epistle (1 Cor. 5:6-8), the church cele-brates the feast of the Paschal Lamb, being called by His already completed sacrifice to be purged of the old influence of self-salvation and to eat the "unleavened bread of sincerity and truth."

The church is constituted by God's calling her out of death into life in union with Jesus Christ. She is literally "the called out" ones.[8] As radical and decisive as is Christ's resurrection, so radically and decisively is the church called into a new existence by the proclama-tion of the Gospel and the hearing of faith.

The church's character as "the called" dare not lead us to assume that once having been called by the Gospel and raised to the new life of faith, the church now proceeds to live by some logical or litur-gical description of her own calledness. The church does not receive an autonomous life, as if a deposit of heavenly U-235 had been stored in her which now radiates a kind of heavenly energy to those around her. The church's churchly (that is, "calledness") character is that God continues to call her and she continues to hear. Worship is the continuing activity of the church, preaching the Gospel to hear it, hearing the Gospel to speak it, that God might continue to be He who constitutes her and she be constantly re-formed in the image of Christ her Lord.

All this is not to say that the church has no history or continuity, as if she arose like a stalagmite, sheer and surd out of the surface of humanity. God the caller and the church's nature as the called constitute the rock and the ground of the continuity. The church is held in shape by Christ the Keystone; she is built on the foundation

---

[7] Cf. Ap XXIV 71—73 (Tappert, p. 262), where the mortification/vivifica-tion transaction is related to the proper, i. e., faithful, use of the Sacrament of the Altar.

[8] The technically trained reader will recognize the double use of the word "called out." For others it should be noted that the Greek word for church, *ek-klesia,* is literally the "called out" ones. This semantic advantage is used extensively in this essay to underscore the activity of God in calling men, in the worship activity of the church as she participates in this divine activity, and in the called being not only addressees but also mouthpieces of the call.

of the apostles and prophets. It follows from this that the worship of the church is always confessional in character.[9] She ever magnifies the name of the Lord and exults in Him as her dwelling place, because He has called her out of darkness into His marvelous light. Furthermore, all her worship, both in words and actions, is normed by the apostolic and prophetic Word. In every gathering of the church for worship, whether in the assembly around preaching the Gospel and administering the Sacrament or in the devotions of a family around the table, there is an inner structure by which God carries out the ministry of the Word of reconciliation.[10]

At worship the unity of the church is created and revealed. This assertion is an attempt to expound Article VII of the Augsburg Confession. The unity of the church does not arise from the similarity of rites and ceremonies, since "it is sufficient for the true unity of the Christian church that the Gospel be preached in conformity with a pure understanding of it and that the sacraments be administered in accordance with the divine Word."[11] Significantly, the stress of Article VII is on "preaching" and "administering," descriptions of the congregation of saints in action. Those who are called by God's Gospel are set in motion to call others and to administer to each other. The unity of the church is created and revealed in this calling. God gathers men by calling them, and the calling goes on in the world through human mouths and language. Hence the unity of the Christians with each other lies in their faithfully calling one another on behalf of God to be reconciled to God through Christ. The church strives to keep the unity by striving to hear, to receive, to communicate, and to serve this call. Since the Gospel is about the will of God's love, the called not only strive to proclaim but also to live the calling: The called *are* what they are called. (See 1 John 3:1-3)

---

[9] See Hans Kressel, *Wilhelm Löhe als Liturg und Liturgiker* (Neuendettelsau: Freimund Verlag, 1952), pp. 52—80. The first principle Kressel lists as the basis of Löhe's liturgical thinking is, "Lutherische Liturgik muss bekenntnissgebunden sein." Ibid., p. 63.

[10] Professor Caemmerer has treated this theme extensively, with his typical creativeness and chiseled style. See, for example, *Feeding and Leading* (St. Louis: Concordia Publishing House, 1962), especially ch. 1; *The Church in the World* (St. Louis: Concordia Publishing House, 1949; 3d printing revised, 1961), passim; and *Preaching for the Church* (St. Louis: Concordia Publishing House, 1959), especially Part I. His essay "The Practice of Holy Communion," *The Abiding Word*, III (St. Louis: Concordia Publishing House, 1960), 531—61, is one treatment of this theme by him which has not received enough attention.

[11] AC VII 2 (Tappert, p. 32).

The church at worship receives, shares, and learns her holiness. Her holiness is not to be sought in her piety or in her deeds. In fact, Jesus' words make it quite plain that we do not have access to an unambiguous distinction between the "good works" of Christians and pagans. And if the good works of Christians, which men see them do, are to be stimulants for glorifying the Father, then those good works themselves need to be illuminated. The light which lightens the church and makes her members lights in the world is the light which they themselves are to let shine "that they [men] may see your good works and give glory to your Father who is in heaven" (Matt. 5:16). What is this light but the Gospel of Jesus Christ's work for the salvation of sinners by forgiving them and sustaining them in the light of the grace of God in the face of Jesus Christ? (cf. 2 Cor. 3 and 4). The "called" are those "called to be saints" (1 Cor. 1:2), and the holiness of those saints is given and received in that work which the Spirit does, when and where He pleases,[12] through the spoken Word when He both gives the salvation described and also stimulates into life the faith which receives that salvation. The church at worship receives and shares her holiness.

The church really shares the holiness. She participates in it, for she is united to the Holy One. The Gospel, which the church hears in speaking, predicates holiness of those who receive it by faith. In predicating holiness by the Gospel, the Spirit gives Christ in His saving victory to those who believe. By faith through the Gospel the church is united with Christ and bound to Him. What is said of Christ in the Gospel is said of those who receive Him in faith. The sacraments are signs of this transaction among the Christians, binding the saints together to Christ in holiness. So radically are the called made sharers in that saving work of God that the church herself becomes part of the sign of the holiness given by God's calling her and by her worshipfully (faithfully) receiving His call. As the sacraments are the signs of God's gracious presence, doing among the Christians what He promises in Christ, so the community of the called and the works done in union with Christ are signs to stimulate the called to firmer, bolder work.[13]

---

[12] Cf. AC V (Tappert, p. 31).

[13] On the similarity between the signs of God's gracious presence in the sacraments and the signs of the Christian life, compare Ap IV 276 (Tappert, p. 148). For the Latin text, *Die Bekenntnisschriften der evangelisch-lutherischen Kirche*, 2. verb. Auf. (Göttingen: Vandenhoeck & Ruprecht, 1952), pp. 214 ff.

Without worship (that is, without faith receiving this "Spirited" work of God) the church has no holiness. The holiness that men see in the religious man or in the religious community is precisely human holiness, holiness produced by man, subject to empirical investigation. But the holiness of the church at worship is a reality of the believing community as well as of the individual. Because this reality escapes the empirical scrutiny of man and is rather posited in the calling, it does not by that token turn into an ideal or an inner relationship of each one with the holy. Holiness is "given" in worship. It is shared. From it all else is sanctified, "for everything created by God is good, and nothing is to be rejected if it is received with thanksgiving; for then it is consecrated by the Word of God and prayer" (1 Tim. 4:4-5). Nor is the holiness of the church to be spiritualized into a vapor of sentiment and good intention. That it is worked by the Holy Spirit in and through the called does not make it nonmaterial. In baptizing and in celebrating the Holy Eucharist, the Word of God is most explicitly united to people and things, calling people to be washed and to be fed on holy food. What the church eats she becomes, not on the grounds of her activity but in her worship. That is, she receives in faith what God gives and what He does. From this center of "communion in holy things"[14] the whole life of the church at worship moves out. To this center all returns.

In worship the catholicity of the church is effected, practiced, and disclosed. God's will in Christ is to make the called blessed "with every spiritual blessing in the heavenly places" (Eph. 1:3). The wholeness which God confers in the fullness of His love in Christ is by the redemption through the blood of Jesus Christ. All wisdom and insight are disclosed in Christ to illuminate the mystery of God's will "to unite all things in Him [Christ], things in heaven and things on earth" (Eph. 1:10). The revelation of this purpose and its achievement in and through the church actually happen as God's work when the Gospel is heard and believed (Eph. 1:11-13) and those believing hearers are sealed by the promised Holy Spirit. It is this receiving

(hereafter cited as *BKS*). Note especially Luther's marginal comment, *BKS*, p. 214, note 2. On the church as the arena of the Spirit's sanctifying activity, see LC, Creed, 35—37 (Tappert, p. 415), and especially, Creed, 51—56 (Tappert, pp. 417—18). On the usage of sacraments as signs, as understood in this essay, see also Ap XXIV 69—70 (Tappert, p. 262).

14 For this interpretation of *communio sanctorum* see Werner Elert, *Abendmahl und Kirchengemeinschaft in der alten Kirche, hauptsächlich des Ostens* (Berlin: Lutherisches Verlagshaus, 1954), pp. 166—81.

the Gospel in the seal of the Spirit that is worship, worship in spirit and truth.

The catholicity of the church resides in Christ, her Head, in whose resurrection from the dead God accomplished the conquest of all divisive powers and authorities. This same immeasurable greatness of power is at work in those who believe. Their believing is the worshipful living in which they cry out in thanksgiving and call out in intercession, to be illumined to see Him as Head of all. Their worship is the outpouring of their already answered desire to become the fullness of Him who fills all in all. (Eph. 1:15-23)

Wholeness is both life and unity. By "catholicity" the called posit the reality of the full rescue from the wrath of God and from death. They proclaim and live as the new creation which is already under way, a new people productive of good works in God's ordained activity in creation. Catholicity asserts that in the called both the religious and nonreligious are reconciled into one new man, by the preaching of Jesus Christ.[15] The whole company of the called is bound together in time and space, and indwelt by God. In that company are included all of every time and place who hear and receive the "Spirited" Gospel. In turn, the church (that is, the called) herself becomes part of God's display of His will to the entire cosmos, "that through the church the manifold wisdom of God might now be made known to the principalities and powers in the heavenly places." (Eph. 3:10)

The church at worship is the church cultivating the life in God. Cultic activity — liturgy, with its action, in the specific sense — is that conduct in specific ways, places, times, and forms by which the called cultivate this life in God. They discipline, guard, and foster this life in each other by being the "calling" people. Their calling is not merely a status; it is an activity. They are calling all life into participation and conformity to the life of those called out of darkness into His marvelous light. (1 Peter 2:9)

The church's worship is her vocation. In the following material the stress will be on "vocation" as the "calling activity," with the word construed as the form of an active participle more than as a noun. The subject for exploration is the church at worship, with

---

[15] See Eph. 2. "Religious and nonreligious" are used as paraphrases for Jew and Gentile.

this activity of the "called" described primarily as their "calling to" one another and to the world. Both the cultic, liturgical life and the life of common work will be treated.

It has been asserted that the real battle in the life of worship is the conflict between faith and idolatry. If this is so, it follows that the chief threat to true worship is the snatching of the Gospel from the heart and mouth and ears of the called, and raising barriers to prevent one from calling out to another in the name of Jesus Christ, calling each other to be reconciled and renewed. The barriers can be of a wide variety, from the most destructive activity of distorting the Gospel [16] to the hateful and self-seeking heart of the worshipers; [17] from self-satisfied indifference to chaotic gibberish of one sort or another which prevents one Christian from uttering the Word of the Gospel to another in such a way that the other can comprehend it. (Cf., for example, 1 Cor. 14)

Worship is that activity in which the ascended Christ reigns in His temple, preserving the called not only in union with Himself but also in unity with each other. He who is called the Son of God (for so He is) came down from heaven to become the Founder and Life-giver of the new humanity of the Last Age. He ascended on high, leading captivity captive.[18] His calling His people is the beginning of their life, and their living is a "walking worthy of the calling to which [they] . . . have been called." The calling is constitutive of their unity as the community of the Last Time. Each one of them seeks to keep the unity of the calling by living the life of the calling. Their life is a calling each other in and to the Gospel. Unity with the ascended Christ is unity with the victory that overthrows captivity. Striving to keep the unity of the Spirit in the bond of peace is continuing in the calling. The church at worship is the church keeping the unity, walking as the called and calling people.

Each of the members of the church is "graced" according to the measure of Christ's gift (Eph. 4:7). To equip and to train the called

16 This real danger helps to account for the indispensable place of dogma in the life of the church. Furthermore, this danger calls for serious attention to be given to Jesus' warnings to beware of false prophets (Matt. 7:7-28, a section which involves much discussion of "worship activity"). This danger also emphasizes the appropriateness of all worship activity as a call to repent. On the first item, see Jaroslav Pelikan, "The Functions of Theology," *Theology in the Life of the Church*, ed. Robert W. Bertram (Philadelphia: Fortress Press, 1963), pp. 3—21.

17 The sort of thing Paul treats extensively in 1 Cor. 10—13.

18 Eph. 4:8. What follows is based chiefly on Eph. 4:1—6:19.

in their calling, the ascended Christ gives gifts: some apostles, some prophets, some evangelists, some pastors and teachers. These men, themselves called into a unique function for service to the saints, equip the saints for the ministry, a ministry aimed at the growth and maturity of the whole company of the called so that the entire body grows up to full manhood to be formed in the image of Christ. Negatively, such training guards the called from mortally deceptive opinions and from childish immaturity. Positively, such diaconic activity of the saints is carried on by "truthing one another in love" [19] into Christ.

The cultus, liturgical form and action, plays an essential role in this service of "speaking the truth in love." "The purpose of observing ceremonies is that men may learn the Scriptures and that those who have been touched by the Word may receive faith and fear and so may also pray." [20] The liturgy and its forms are the grammar and syntax for each one in the worshiping community to exercise his unique place in the priestly activity of hearing the Word from and speaking the Word to his neighbor. The forms are avenues so that each may have an open, uncluttered approach for common praise and intercession, for magnifying the name of God to the person next to him, and conjointly to the world. The cult is for cultivating the priestly community in hearing the reconciling call of God as it issues from the mouth of the calling people. Cultus as form is as necessary for the courteous dialog in worship as are grammar and syntax for lucid and coherent speech. The center of the cult (the Word and water in baptizing, the spoken Word in absolution and in preaching remission of sins, the Word with bread and wine and the Lord's body and blood) can never be safeguarded or shared without cultic form and action. While no particular liturgical form is given to God's church, these works of God at the center of the church's worship are themselves creative of new forms; and these same works of God are normative over the forms used. Ceremonies are for the sake of the Word of God and for the sake of those who are to hear it in faith, full of awe and with prayer. The function of the form is to safeguard the use of that Word.

The form is like the husk on an ear of corn. Only a man igno-

[19] Eph. 4:15. This wording is Professor Caemmerer's. Although the phrasing is awkward in English, it does lay stress in the participle ἀληθεύοντες.

[20] Ap XXIV 3 (Tappert, p. 250).

rant of the life and growth of corn would conclude that since nothing but the kernels of corn are eaten, one can raise corn without the bother of husks. On the other hand, it would be a fool indeed who, seeing the necessity of the husk, would after the ear was full grown throw away the ear and eat the husk.

The liturgical forms and ceremonial actions are for the sake of the Gospel, that it may be spoken and heard, that it may be believed, and that God may be praised by men. Forms stand against chaos and willfulness in the congregation. Forms stand against sentimental slosh being passed off as worship. But forms also stand as open avenues, common and known to the users, by which each one has a publicly defined way to speak and hear the Gospel. In so doing, he becomes the glass to magnify the name of God to the others.

The congregation's liturgical forms are communal in nature. They arise from the life, spirit, and activity of the community. They serve the cultivation of life and its growth in the community of the Spirit. They are expressions of the unity and continuity of the whole congregation of God on earth and in heaven. They do not constitute the unity. Unity is in the Gospel by which Christ is present by the Spirit. But forms express the unity in hearing and speaking the Gospel, and forms afford each member of the priestly people the open road for "striving to keep the unity of the Spirit" in the Gospel.

While the pragmatic test is the basic norm for forms, it is not the sole norm. It is precisely the freedom of faith that liberates the worshiping Christians to practice the humility of submitting to the forms as an expression of servant love to the neighbor.[21] The creation of forms is charismatic, either for an individual or for the body. The revision of forms is part of the freedom of those who are the freeborn in the Spirit. For these reasons only those who are charismatically endowed are to create the new forms for worship, either as the creative impulse or the need arises. And only those who are called to exercise the pastoral authority publicly are to revise the forms, for the use and revision of form is a profoundly pastoral act and must be carried out for this goal and to this service.

The renewal of the church, so far as human agents volitionally cooperate with the Spirit of God, arises in and from the church at worship. None other than the Gospel, the oral, audible, and edible

---

[21] Compare the brilliant paragraph on the humility that is able to submit to and use ritual in C. S. Lewis, *Preface to Paradise Lost* (London: Oxford University Press, 1942), pp. 15 ff.

Word about Jesus Christ's death for us and His resurrection as our Peace with God, can furnish the "Spirited" impulse for renewal. And the very heart of pastoral care is the central concern of the called and ordained servant of the Word that the called hear God calling them, continue to live as those who hear, and go on calling to each other. The liturgical forms of the congregation's gathered worship are the focal point of renewal, keeping open communal access to the fountainhead. Each calls the other to stand under the Gospel in that faith which is the loss of his deceit and sin. Each calls the other to willingly submit his self-will to God's will and his self-love to the love of the neighbor. Each calls the other to the loss of death and refuse for the gain of life, for the Gospel spoken and heard bequeathes the life it describes. To walk in the calling is to be renewed, having been undone in the union with Christ's death. The baptismal immersion of the old Adam day by day, slaying him by contrition and confession, and the revival of life in the forgiveness of sins through faith by hearing the absolution, eating the bread of remembrance, and drinking the chalice of salvation are designedly the exercise of pastoral care in calling, which is continued in that care-full calling to each other by the called.

The liturgical forms and actions are public instruments for such caring in calling. They are the training ground for "gospeling" each other and being "gospeled." Obviously, ritual can become ritualism. But the conquest of ritualism is neither formlessness nor an infinite variation of forms. The overthrow of ritualism, like the destruction of any other idolatry, is brought about by the advent of the true God; that is, by the Gospel. True worship is always its own reformation.[22]

22 It is clear that the worship service is here conceived as being pedagogical but not *merely* didactic. The liturgy certainly is discipline: The disciples of the Lord are being disciplined in the life of the cross of Jesus Christ, and are disciplining each other. For a good discussion of this "pedagogical vs. re-presentational" view of the worship service, see Vajta (note 1 above), pp. 33 ff. (German), pp. 19 ff. (English). He argues that what I have called *merely* didactic is based on a misunderstanding of Luther's theological polarities: God/faith. By its very structure Vajta's entire book reveals a continual dialog on this question: Part I, "Worship as the Work of God"; Part II, "Worship as the Work of Faith." Three other studies on the relation of cultus to the Gospel, each covering different periods and serving different goals, are helpful. One is Ernst Lohmeyer, *The Lord of the Temple: A Study of the Relation Between Cult and Gospel,* trans. Steward Todd (Edinburgh and London: Oliver and Boyd, 1961), especially ch. 1, in which he states the problem. The second is Friedrich Kalb, *Theology of Worship in 17th-Century Lutheranism,* trans. Henry P. A. Hamann (St. Louis: Concordia Publishing House, 1965), especially Part II, pp. 67 ff. The third is Vilmos Vajta, "Theological Basis and Nature of the Liturgy," *Lutheran World,* VI (December 1959), 3, 234—46.

The church at worship, however, is not coterminal with the church gathered for worship services. The unity constituted by the calling Gospel and the unity maintained by the called themselves calling each other bind the church into a web, a net of care, which is cast out into humanity and into the world of work. The life of the church is the new life in Christ which interpenetrates not only the old life with its darkness within the believers; but, by way of the Christians, this life also interpenetrates the common life of the world. Yet the interpenetration is not merely individualist assaults on sectors of the world. The called are constituted into a unity: In the Spirit, by the Gospel, they are tied to each other in a web of love and care for the world and for the work which they carry out in the world. They themselves are a reclaimed segment of history and creation. Each is a hallowed part of the new creation. The call of God which makes them the church hallows them. As they themselves are hallowed and constituted by this calling, they hallow their life and work by that calling.

It is striking how much reference to "talk" there is in Ephesians, especially ch. 4. Not only does the apostle call the Christians "to speak the truth in love" in relation to the vocational unity of the church, but he also urges those who are "members of one another" to speak the truth to each other in the relationships that have to do with daily life together. He ties their "truth talk" to such things as anger, work, and their entire attitude toward each other in the friction of daily give and take (Eph. 4:25-32). Falsehood is to be put away. Truth is to be spoken. The apostle's concern is that clean, grace-giving talk come out of the Christians' mouths so that he who hears may be edified. Paul's vocabulary ("edification," "grace") indicates the language of worship and cultus. His concern is not merely "truthfulness" as the moral abstinence from saying things to the neighbor which do not correspond to the facts. Rather, his care is that unity be established and maintained between the members of the called. The tool for achieving this unity is the truth, not merely talk congruent with the facts, but the truth of the calling, the talk of life in God through Christ which is itself the content of one calling to the other one in truth. The talk must be designed to fit the occasion, to grace the hearer. God's call to be reconciled to Him is the very call which the called issue as in forbearance they seek to reconcile the hardheartedness, violence, bitterness, and wrath which arise from the frictions of daily life together. They are themselves the called people engaged in calling. They are calling to imitate Christ.

Such "imitation of Christ" is the church at worship, both in the focused center of the liturgical service and in the dispersed positions of daily life and work. Bound to God in Jesus Christ as she shares Him in His offered benefits, the church celebrates the victorious presence and awaits the appearance of the Lord Jesus. Her very life is cruciform, for she celebrates Christ's death as her death to sin and His resurrection as her own new life. She has the courageous humility to accept God's just judgment of death, and she is expectantly awaiting renewal in life eternal as God calls her from death. Her worship is her activity of copying God, as dear children (Eph. 5:1-2). As she is made alive in God's love through the self-giving of Jesus Christ, who by His sacrifice perfumes her with the divine pleasure of His sacrifice, she lives in love, giving her life for those around her who have only the smell of death. Such love is the nature of the life she lives, for it is the nature of the life God gives.

The Word of God by which she is called out of death into life with the Son of God — and therefore the Word by which she continues her calling, her life as church — links together the church at worship in the cultus with the church at worship in the common life. The church has no sacred autonomy by which she sanctifies the common life. Neither does she live in a religious or nonreligious secularity, as a self-enclosed sphere whereby what she does is automatically construed as godly. She cannot, in some enthusiasm for the world, presuppose the Gospel in the name of a nature/grace continuum. Neither can she, in her enthusiasm for the Gospel, abandon the world in its common life. The Word of the cross, which constitutes her hallowed peace and sacred unity in the worship of God in the cultic service, is the Word that gives her the shape of her life in the world. By this Word the relationships in creation and the life of work in the world are bound in unity to the holy peace.[23] As by the Word of the Gospel (both in audible and sacramental form) God calls the church to participate in the death of Christ offered on the altar of the cross, so Christians, by taking this Word in their mouths and calling it out to each other, offer up their lives in suffering and death on the altar of their daily work. The Word of God

[23] Compare the excellent study on this point in Regin Prenter, "Luther's Theology of the Cross," *Lutheran World,* VI (December 1959), 3, 222—33.

binds the church's daily life to the cross of Christ. The celebration of Christ's victory through His death and resurrection "for us" is the participation in that death and resurrection by God's calling. That worship which is life is participation in Christ by faith. Such participation occurs not only in the liturgical service and sacramental usage. It occurs also as the death of man appears and occurs in the common tasks of life. In those places too, the called celebrate the victory of Christ by calling upon God and calling their work back to God. The church is constituted by God's calling in every place where this call is received. Hearing it, the called sanctify their own life and work by "calling" it God's.

With the finger of His Spirit God is writing in the church a "carbon copy" of the original Word, the Word He wrote in Christ. The pattern of the church's continuing "imitation of God as dear children" [24] guides the church in throwing off immorality, impurity, and covetousness by means of thanksgiving. Rather than be deceived by "empty words," the church is to be filled with the words which commemorate the work of Christ, for thanksgiving is essentially a rehearsal of God's work and words. Empty words provoke the wrath of God; the words of thanksgiving illuminate Christians, making them shine in the darkling world. Being lighted, they are called to shine as lights. The darkness in the world, which Christians are to dispel, is not a darkness of the lack of electricity, nor an absence of scientific and cultural knowledge. Rather, it is a darkness in men's minds and hearts which drives men to spend all their time and energies in the compulsive bondage of self-authentication, the drive to overcome God's just judgment of death on their whole lives. The darkness of the world is idolatry — that worship which is death. It is a darkness which shows itself just as readily in gazing up over a launching pad into space as it does in bowing down before a totem pole.

In this wilderness of darkness, where death reigns by the absence of light, in this "Heart of Darkness" (to use Conrad's title), the church is called to shine as lights. The light which lightens her and gives her life is God's calling her into Jesus Christ. Therefore the church, with this Gospel in her heart and mouth, is God's voice crying in the wilderness, calling men away from their unbelief, calling to

[24] Eph. 5:1. The discussion which follows is based on and shaped by Eph. 5:1—6:9.

men in order to illuminate them with the work of God in their common life.[25] God's Word is always given to people through people. The church is at worship as she hears and receives, as she gives thanks and speaks this Word. With her ongoing participation in God's calling, the church is wise, "buying up the time," literally turning every day and every night of her life back to God the Creator. Whereas the world robs God by using time and creation for its own self, fighting to oppose the just judgment of God, the church in time and in creation joins the will of God to overthrow evil. Her instrument for extricating the evil is God's instrument: the Word of God. Hence the apostle urges the church to join God's will as the segment of the new creation in the world, to be filled with the Spirit by "addressing one another in psalms and hymns and spiritual songs" (Eph. 5:19), and with melodious hearts to give thanks always. God's activity in worship, in which the church joins by faith, is the overthrow of idolatry (the will to save one's own life) and the dispelling of darkness (the enslaving opinion that one must and can save himself). By her thanksgiving the church does nothing more and nothing less than remember Christ's victory by rehearsing the story of it, sharing it in eating and drinking the Eucharist, and taking the call of God into her own mouth to call it to the world.

The church at worship may be compared to the activity in a camp of soldiers preparing for battle. The call to battle is given. Soldiers share it by calling to one another, urging each other to preparation and courage, clothing each other for battle and victory. Thus the called clothe each other in the truth, equipping each other with that one weapon for the offense: the sword of the Spirit, which is the Word of God. The church's desire that this instrument may be used effectively is poured out in prayer "at all times in the Spirit, with all prayer and supplication" that each one may open his mouth boldly to speak the "mystery of the Gospel." (Eph. 6:18-19)

The church at worship is called to offer sacrifices *to* God. Such sacrifices are offered *for* the neighbor. The life of "living sacrifice" (Rom. 12:1) is rooted in the "mercies of God." The living of the sacrifice is the "spiritual worship," those called presenting their bodies in the steadfast continuation of the calling. By the Gospel God not only reveals the mystery of Christ. He also takes the church out

25 Cf. Luther's expression in the "Formula Missae": "Quod Euangelion sit vox clamans in deserto et vocans ad fidem infideles . . ." *D. Martin Luthers Werke* (Weimar, 1891), XII, 211. See also LC, Creed, 51 (Tappert, p. 417).

of death into the unity with Christ (see Eph. 1 and 3). In the mystery of the Gospel God joins both the religious and irreligious into that one body which itself becomes part of the disclosure of the mystery of God's will to the whole cosmos (Eph. 3:7-13). The life that is given to those who are thus joined to the sacrifice of Christ is the life of faith. As has been said, such faith is the highest worship of God. It follows, as Apology XXIV argues,[26] that the highest sacrifice the church offers is preaching and celebrating that Word by which God has united the church already in the forgiveness of sins in Jesus Christ. The real, daily sacrifice is that "proclamation and the faith which truly believes that by the death of Christ God has been reconciled." [27]

From the central activity of worship as receiving in faith the offered reconciliation in Christ, which creates the new life in her, the church derives boldness from that very Word of God which she hears while speaking. Her courage is the joy of offering all her suffering to God, not only as pleasing to Him but also as the manifestation of the victory of His gracious will over evil. She does not call suffering an act to propitiate God, but by calling out in proclamation and prayer, the church rejoices in her union with the Mediator, in consort with whom she is instrumental in bearing some specific piece of evil in the world. She accepts the death inflicted on her, not in morbidity but in union with Christ's conquering death. At worship one Christian calls to another with the remembrance of Christ's sufferings that each together may turn over all suffering to God as a joyful celebration of God's victory in Christ.

In a similar way the church offers all her work in creation as a sacrifice to God. She does not do this by some false notion of dividing secular and sacred work. Nor does she live in a romantic dream which bases the holiness of work on the motives and sense of fulfillment of the worker. This is not because the church has no distinctions between secular and sacred, nor is it that she has no concern about motives and human fulfillment. Rather, it is because the Word which has called her "holy" is the Word by which she sanctifies the whole life. Her continuing holiness in her entire life — making sacred everything men ordinarily view as autonomous — is her ongoing activity of calling with the voice of God's Gospel to the whole life of

---

[26] Tappert, pp. 249—68; *BKS,* pp. 349—77.

[27] Ap XXIV 38 (Tappert, p. 257).

each other, giving the common work into the completion of God's will to eradicate evil from the created world. Into the very structures established and maintained in the created world by the Creator and Judge, the called interpenetrate the common relationships. Just as men use these structures to carry out their evil and to inflict their self-will (to the extent they are able) on others, so the called, as that web of God's caring people, use these structures to absorb the evil. By the Gospel they unite it to Christ's suffering and celebrate the victory of Christ through the servant love to the people around them. The voluntary submission of spouses to each other, the network of care in the parent-children relationship, the discipline in family and work to offer service to God, the approach to people for serving them, which is afforded through government and voluntary agencies, are not sentimental mouthings. These structures are the very places where the called offer their lives in sacrifice to God for the neighbor; they are the places where the church, receiving the call to join Christ's victorious death and resurrection, lives out the will of God by calling all self-will and self-love into death with Christ. And, in the selfsame structures, the called live out toward the neighbor that love of God which they share in their union with Christ. They celebrate the resurrection of Christ in their works of love. As the saints are consecrated to God by His calling them beloved sons in the Beloved Son, so in that same calling their works are consecrated to God. As they continue to live their calling, the saints turn their specific part of the created world back into repossession by God through their lordship over it.[28]

The church at worship is ruled by the call of God's Gospel. In her life in the world the church joins God in exercising rule over the created world by calling it God's and offering it freely in God's name to do God's assigned task in the world.

[28] See the excellent article by Regin Prenter, "Worship and Creation," *Studia Liturgica,* II (June 1963), 2, 82—93.

PART III

"What is the core? the rallying point?"

CHAPTER 6

Is There a Lutheran Hermeneutics?

EDWARD H. SCHROEDER

Is there a distinctively Lutheran interpretation of the Scriptures? In his recent book *The Holy Spirit and Modern Thought*, Lindsay Dewar (an Anglican) says the answer is Yes. At least in Luther himself, says he, there is a distinctive and unique hermeneutics at work — *and it is a bad one.*

> Luther was essentially a man of one idea; and that idea was Justification by Faith. . . . It is this "one-track-mindedness" which makes Luther so unsatisfactory as a Biblical commentator, despite his phenomenal knowledge of the text of the Scriptures. And it was this which gave the Reformation at the outset such an unfortunate theological bias. . . . "Exegesis was not Luther's strong point, and his commentaries bristle with faults. They are defective and prolix; full of bitter controversy and one-sided." [1]

It is my contention that Canon Dewar is right in his insight into Luther's "one-sided" interpretation of the Scriptures, but I think the one-sidedness is commendable.

In this chapter I want to dwell a bit on Luther's way of interpreting the Scriptures and then to look at the Lutheran Confessions as collected in *The Book of Concord,* specifically the fourth article of the Apology of the Augsburg Confession, in order to get at what is unique and distinctive in the Lutheran interpretation of Scripture.

Even though Lutherans are not bound to Luther, we must devote

[1] Lindsay Dewar, *The Holy Spirit and Modern Thought* (New York, 1959), p. 125.

some attention to this one-sidedness of Luther, because it directly affects the statements of the later Confessions on the way Scripture ought to be used and the way the Confessions themselves actually do use the Bible as they go about interpreting it.

I. LUTHER

The starting point for the Reformation in Western Catholicism was an exegetical discovery by a man whose official title was "doctor of the Holy Scriptures." His discovery centered on the meaning of the Biblical term "righteousness of God." (In English the word *righteousness* does not normally call to mind the word *justification,* because many of our English words come from a Latin family tree and many others from the Anglo-Saxon. But in the native tongues of the German Reformation the two terms automatically go together and almost sound like each other: in German, *Rechtfertigung* and *Gerechtigkeit;* and in Latin, *justitia* and *justificatio.)*

It was initially in his lecturing to students on the Psalms and then later in his lectures on Romans that the Biblical answer came to Luther's question: What is the "righteousness of God"? Medieval theology had taught him correctly that no man can stand before God (neither today nor on the Last Day) unless he have God's own righteousness. And the general conclusion was: Get busy! But Luther's great discovery was that God wants to give me that very necessary righteousness as a present, gratis, so that I can indeed stand muster before Him, not only on the Last Day but every day of my life from here to eternity. The name of that gratuitous present of God's own righteousness is Jesus Christ. So the "surprise" of Christianity, the unexpected Good News, is that although men do have to have God's righteousness, the righteousness is gratis, *sola gratia.* The name of this surprise — this secret, marvel, mystery, and wonder which no one ever could have guessed — is Jesus Christ. Hence, *solus Christus.* The mode by which the free gift becomes my gift is the *faithfulness* of God which evokes my trust *(sola fides).* Consequently for Luther "righteousness of God," "Jesus Christ," and "justification by grace through faith" are all synonymns. They all refer to the one heart of the entire matter of Christianity.

If we have everything else in the Christian heritage, all the other articles of faith, but do not have this, we have nothing. At least, we have nothing specifically Christian to stand on. The opposite is also true. So long as we still have this one gratis gift, we may let every-thing else go — "life, goods, fame, child, and wife" — and we have not lost out on anything. In practice Luther applied this line from "A Mighty Fortress" to theology itself. If a supposed article of faith has nothing to do with this one article, it will become a competitor with the *solus Christus*. Whatever we let go without letting go of this one gracious gift is no real loss; we are still fully and truly Christian, and we dare let no one convince us that we are not. If someone tries to do so, he is criticizing not us but our Lord Christ — the conse-quences of which, for the critic, are disastrous.

As far as the history of Western Christian theology was con-cerned, Luthers' discovery brought St. Paul's theology of the righteous-ness of God back into the center of theological conversation after a very long hibernation. Thus it is no surprise when the Lutheran Confessions in the following years give prime attention to this theol-ogy of God's righteousness. But here something happens which Joachim Beckmann calls unique in the history of Christian theology up until that time.[2] The Lutheran confessors do not say: Here is one important element in the total package of Christian theology that has been lost, a brick that has fallen out of the edifice of Christian the-ology, and we now desire to have it put back where it belongs so that the package may be complete. They do not treat this as one article among the several important articles of faith, but they confess that it is the *only* article of faith. Even when we read the confessors' discussions of other articles, we soon become aware that in all their varied assertions and affirmations they have only one confession, one article, which stands out as the recurring and monotonous theme under all the variations. Later it was even called "the article by which the church stands or falls" *(articulus stantis et cadentis ecclesiae)*. Medi-eval theology before the Reformation (at least all the way back to Augustine and perhaps all the way back to the so-called "apostolic fathers" of the early second century) had considered the Christian faith to be composed of many articles, gathered together, e. g., in the creed, and drawn from the Holy Scriptures. At the very least, there were *three* articles of faith as represented by the three articles of the creed. Others saw the Apostles' Creed itself as containing at least 12 articles (one from each apostle), all of which were part of the

---

[2] Here and elsewhere below are reflected perspectives formulated in Joachim Beckmann, "Die Bedeutung der reformatorischen Entdeckung des Evangeliums für die Auslegung der Heiligen Schrift," *Luther*, XXXIV (1963), 20—30.

total Christian package. The articles of faith presented in the creed were articles of *faith* because God had revealed them in the Holy Scriptures as a *philosophia coelestis.*

This notion that there are numerous articles of faith goes hand in hand with a corresponding notion of what the Bible is. It amounts to something like this: The Bible is the source book for all the things God has revealed for the heavenly philosophy, which Christians acknowledge in the numerous things (articles) that they confess as being and belonging to the Christian faith. Since the Lutherans shifted the concept of Christian theology from numerous articles of faith to one and only one basic and foundational article, we ought not be surprised when they also make a shift in their understanding of the Scriptures. The shift can be seen in the actual use they make of this Book. It still functions as source, of course, but a source unique and different from the kind of source book it had been for theology up until that time. Let us now try to see how the Reformation discovery resulting from Luther's study of the Bible affected what Lutherans say about the Bible.

The Reformation discovery of the one article of faith in all Christian theology led the Reformers to a renewed concentration on the Bible. There had been important Biblical work in preceding centuries, but the Reformers had a distinctive reason for getting back to the Bible. Their distinctive reason, by the way, was not their conviction of the plenary verbal inspiration of the Bible, which of course they did acknowledge. The Reformers' distinctive reason for getting back to the Bible was a bit roundabout. Joachim Beckmann traces the sequence as follows: With the rediscovery of the Gospel of the righteousness of God *(gratia, Christus, fides),* verbal communication of this gift of God becomes the central means of grace. The term *Word of God* designates the one central means of grace whereby the gift is transmitted to people, whereby the benefits of Christ are conveyed to the intended beneficiaries. This phrase, *Word of God,* is used synonymously with the word *Gospel,* and when the Reformers use it they are not thinking first of all of the book called the Bible. In fact in the Smalcald Articles when Luther is mentioning the many forms in which this one Word of God comes to people, he mentions five different forms of this one means of grace, and not one of them is the Scriptures. However, it is the Reformers' conviction of the centrality of this one Word of God (Gospel) which soon sends them back to the Scriptures — but sends them back in a new way with a new question, a question which had not been central to the church's searching of the Scriptures for many centuries, even in the great medieval centers of Biblical studies. The question which the Reformers addressed to the Scriptures was this: What can you tell us about the righteousness of God, which we must have in order to live?

Even the sacraments — which in the medieval church were the chief (if not sole) means of grace — are subsumed in Luther's theology to this one means of grace: Word of God, the verbalized communication of the surprise gift. Thus, for example, in the Small Catechism he says that the words "given and shed for you for the remission of sins" are the chief item in the Eucharist. In place of the priestly sacramental celebrant, the verbally communicating preacher becomes the indispensable professional church worker. Preaching becomes once more, as it had been in the early church, the chief office in the church. The most important consideration in the training of professional church workers is whether or not they know the Gospel and can convey it. This is the chief task of the church. Anything else the professional churchman may have learned before which bypasses this one task is irrelevant and useless. The chief homework of the church in order to get that Gospel known and conveyed is Biblical exegesis. So the chief task of theological education is to teach students of theology (and the laity too) how to work with the Bible, so that God's verbally communicated gift can move out from the Book into the lives of people. That means getting the Word of God (Christ) out of the Word of God (Bible), namely, getting *Him* out of *it*. Consequently, theological education in Wittenberg is restructured to focus on this new center. All validly Christian theological study becomes Biblical study. There is finally no Lutheran theology which is not Biblical theology, but always Biblical study for reasons beyond itself. The Bible is the center of study because of its witness to the primary element in Christianity, the gracious gift. Since there is no other foundation for the church than this one Word of God, there can be no alternative foundation for the church's theology.

The Reformers worked out the consequences of their understanding of the Bible in the conflicts which God brought to them. And we ought not forget that the opponents on the radical left (Anabaptists, *Schwaermer*, Spiritualists, Sacramentarians) were at least as instrumental in forcing the Reformers to some of their convictions as were the Romanists on the right. This is especially true for the Reformers' position on the Scriptures.

Let us turn now to some of the hermeneutic consequences which ensued from the Reformation discovery of the righteousness of God.

1. *Sola Scriptura:* Although this expression is surely one which Luther would have accepted, it achieved greatest prominence among the second-generation Lutherans in their conflicts with the Roman assertion (publicized at Trent) about Scripture *and* tradition. What did the Lutherans mean with *sola scriptura?* Did they want to say that this is the only valid source of doctrine because it is the only inspired source? For Luther at least that was surely not the case. It is not the special inspiration of the Scriptures but the necessity of preaching *solus Christus* which makes him say *sola scriptura.* Since the Biblical Scriptures are the oldest and most original apostolic and prophetic witness to this Christ who is the *solus* content of preaching, therefore they too are characterized as *sola.* Because the Scriptures have the unique character of being the first and most ancient witness to the one Word of God, they cannot be anteceded if one wants to work with sources for the church's one task — verbal communication of the free gift of righteousness. This is why the Scriptures are authoritative. This is why we dare call them Word of God: because the one righteousness of God is contained and conveyed in that original apostolic testimony about Christ. And if it is not, we are lost. We have no access to the Word of God (Him) except the Word of God (it), the witness of the apostles and prophets.

2. *Scriptura sui ipsius interpres* (Scripture is its own interpreter). This sentence is also formulated in confrontation with that Roman tradition which held that the Scriptures are a closed book until the authorized interpreter (ultimately the Roman Pontiff) says what they mean. Luther personally encountered this tradition in his own life, and the subordination of the Scriptures to the ecclesiastical teaching authority had in fact incarcerated the Scriptures. They could no longer say what they wanted to say, but only what the Roman see would let them say. Rome argued that this was necessary because of an *a priori* assumption that the Scriptures were a dark book (cf. Erasmus) and not transparent at all. Luther asserted the contrary: They are clear, simple, transparent. Of course this assertion is directly connected with the one article of the Christian faith which was central to the Reformation discovery: The Scriptures are clear, simple, and trans-

parent in their proclamation concerning the righteousness of God in Jesus Christ. Since that is the central item which God wants to convey to men, it does come across loud and clear in the Scriptures. If we come to Scripture asking the kinds of questions for which the gracious righteousness of God is the answer, then there is no problem in our getting a clear answer. If we come with any other question, then the Scriptures are indeed opaque, dark, and shrouded. When the Lutheran Confessions pick up this notion and talk about "using the clear passages to interpret the difficult ones," they do not mean using the simple sentences to interpret the compound and complicated ones. What they do mean is using the passages which clearly express the one article of righteousness (even though they sometimes are the most complicated sentences grammatically) to get at the meaning of some others which are not so clear — grammatically clear, yes, but not clear in their expression of this one central message.

3. *Christ the Lord of the Scriptures.* In contrast to the Roman assertion that the church was the master of the Scriptures and in contrast to the Enthusiasts' assertion that the internal Spirit was the Lord of all the Scriptures, Luther asserted an audacious one-sided (Canon Dewar is right) concentration on Christ Himself. Christ is the *scopus generalis scripturae,* the actual and eventual target of everything in the Bible, Old Testament included. If it were not for Christ, we would not have a Scripture. He said it Himself in John's gospel. "Searching the Scriptures" has one reason: "They are they which testify of Me." If we are looking for something else in the Scriptures, not only will we have a difficult time with plenty of "dark passages," but we will not even discover the Scriptures at all. A man who reads the Declaration of Independence to discover what colonial English grammar was, may well find an answer to his question, but we would hardly say he had discovered the Declaration of Independence for what it wanted to be. If we succeed in getting a message out of a Biblical text and in doing so avoid hearing or saying something about the one target of all Scripture, God's gracious righteousness in Christ, then we have performed an un-Lutheran exegesis, which in itself is not so bad if it were not for the fact that it is an unbiblical one besides.

Seeing Christ as the Lord of the Scriptures protects one from Biblicism. When the Bible is not viewed as heading for this one sole target, then it becomes a lawbook for doctrines and ethics which is best interpreted by the man who has the most spiritual insight to get the real spirit out of the letters of the words. That is why Biblicism and enthusiastic spiritualism go hand in glove. It takes the Biblical text and interprets and applies it to people's lives without first "forcing" the text to hit the one target (*scopus*) and then picking the text up again, so to speak, "on the rebound." Or one might also say: Biblicism seeks to apply a text directly to human lives without running it through the sieve of Christ, the sieve of the gracious righteousness, without first presenting it before its own Lord.

When Luther is under attack, he can take this conviction of Christ's lordship over the Scriptures and use it in the most impudent fashion, especially in his critical words on certain Biblical texts. On one occasion he says: When the opponents martial the Scriptures against Christ and against the Gospel, I fight back with Christ against the Scriptures. Similarly his words about the "straw epistle" of James and similarly derogatory remarks about other Biblical texts all stem from this conviction. This is the famous *Christum treiben* assertion. Whatever "urges Christ" is the apostolic Word of God, God's gracious righteousness. If it does not do that, then it is not the *apostolic* Word of God — even if it is in the Bible, even if St. Paul himself wrote it, and even if it should qualify on other grounds as an authentic word from God. For *apostolic* Word of God is limited to that which the apostles were authorized to speak by their Lord when He commissioned (*apostello*) them. The mandatory content of that apostolically authorized word is the Commissioner Himself. Hence only *Christum treiben* can qualify as the "apostolic" Word.

4. *The unitary meaning of Scripture.* This is asserted by Luther in contrast to the fourfold meaning of Scripture which he himself, as a product of medieval Biblical scholarship, had practiced. Especially two of these four meanings, the literal and the spiritual (historical and allegorical), had conditioned medieval exegesis ever since Origen. Because Jesus is the tangible historical Word of God in person, therefore the actual, historical, literal meaning of the texts of Scripture conveys to us the one central article of the faith. There is no "spiritual" meaning that is above and beyond or deeper and more concealed than this one historically incarnate Gospel in person. A search for *deus absconditus* behind or beyond *deus revelatus* is not impossible, but is always done at one's own peril. Because the Holy Spirit is the Spirit of the crucified and risen Christ, there is no additional spiritual

meaning that is behind or beyond the actual words and acts of the Word of God incarnate. The exegetical task does not require that I spiritualize the grubby words of the apostles and prophets in order to get back closer to what God *really* wants to say, for God Himself has already done the revealing of what He really wants to say. He has moved His "spiritual" donation into material, historical form so that it (the righteousness) — or better, He (Christ) — can penetrate to us.

In the final analysis the desire somehow to get back through the historical, tangible words and events to a spirit behind them constitutes a vote of no-confidence in God's own revelatory ability. It is an act of *hybris* wherein we presume to penetrate the God-man communication barrier in order to grasp God, thus implying that He cannot get through to us without our help. In Luther's terms this is *theologia gloriae,* the sinful and inordinate lust to view the *deus nudus.* It is a hermeneutical form of original sin. The "mysteries" of God are not hidden behind the words, but they are taken out of hiding simply by what the words literally say of Christ's person and work.

II. THE LUTHERAN CONFESSIONS

All of the above hermeneutical implications regarding Scripture stem from the rediscovered *solus Christus, sola gratia, sola fides.* These are not the three new articles of the Lutheran creed, but three ways of referring to the one righteousness of God, the only one that counts. It is Christ-righteousness and that is all. It is gratis-righteousness and that is all. It is faith-righteousness and that is all. What this rediscovery did for the Reformers' actual interpretation of Scripture can be seen in Article IV of the Apology of the Augsburg Confession. Melanchthon says in these confessional documents that the article of the gracious righteousness of God is the key to the Holy Scriptures. The reason the Roman Catholic critics cannot understand Scripture although they quote it left and right against the Lutherans, is that nowhere in all of their theology do they have this key. Consequently, they cannot be expected to get "inside" the written Word of God.

Lutherans must remember that after the Augsburg Confession was presented in 1530, the Roman response which was soon forthcoming *(Confutatio)* did not quote Thomas and Aristotle to prove that the Lutherans were wrong. Instead, the Roman opponents argued *sola scriptura!* In response to Augustana's Article IV on justification they said, "It is entirely contrary to Holy Scripture to deny that our works are meritorious." "Their [the Lutherans'] ascription of justification to faith alone is diametrically opposed to the truth of the Gospel . . ." That Melanchthon was well aware of this critique from *sola scriptura* which they were making is seen in the preface to his own response to the *Confutatio,* his Apology, where he notes: "Our opponents brag that they have refuted our Confession from the Scriptures." [3] So what we actually have in the whole Apology is the first explicit attempt at stating the Lutheran principles for interpreting Scripture. It is the first expressly Lutheran hermeneutics in action.

This hermeneutics is especially visible in Apology IV, since it was on the doctrinal questions in that article that the opponents thought they had clinched their argument *from Scripture.* Here they cite a wealth of Bible material against the Lutherans. So here Melanchthon is forced to engage in an exegetical debate, not only stating the Lutheran principle of interpretation but actually practicing it, as he countercriticizes the alternative exegesis of his Roman opponents. What constitutes the one article of Christian theology also becomes the one principle and key for interpreting the Scriptures. It is normative for the entire Scriptures from Genesis to Revelation if one wants to understand them the way they themselves wish to be understood. The Reformers' conviction that this was the "sole" principle for going at Scripture was founded partly on the fact that the discovery of its *solus* character in all theology had come from the Scriptures themselves, as Luther had wrestled with them in his lectures on Psalms and Romans. It was *not* a pet idea that Luther had concocted and then tried to apply to the Bible. It was by way of Biblical study that he had been overwhelmed by the heart of God's message to men, the Word of God who is Jesus Christ, the gratuitous righteousness of God. If the heart of the message is this one fundamental article, then any book claiming to be God's Word must also have this one fundamental article as its heart. If the Gospel is the heart of the Bible, then either we have to know this heart ahead of time before we go to study the Scriptures, or we shall have to discover it during the very process of our Scriptural study, or we shall not be getting to the heart of the matter. This makes the Gospel

    [3] *The Book of Concord: The Confessions of the Evangelical Lutheran Church,* trans. and ed. Theodore G. Tappert in collaboration with Jaroslav Pelikan, Robert H. Fischer, and Arthur C. Piepkorn (Philadelphia: Muhlenberg [Fortress] Press, 1959), p. 98.

of the gracious righteousness of God the key to the Scriptures. Without this key we can never really get "in" on what is going on in the Book. We may work around with the Bible all our lives, but without this key it is a closed book.

In Article IV of the Apology, Melanchthon denies that his opponents have this key. They do come to talk about Christ, he says, but the upshot of what they do is to "bury Christ." When they stumble upon the key, they cover it up. They put the resurrected Christ back into the tomb (17 f., 81).[4] At one point Melanchthon says that he is amazed "that our opponents are unmoved by the many passages in the Scriptures that clearly attribute justification to faith," i. e., announce the one and chief article. He wonders whether they perhaps think that "these words fell from the Holy Spirit unawares" (107 f.). After reviewing the "main passages which our opponents quote against us," Melanchthon says in summary that they "maliciously twist the Scriptures to fit their own opinions. They quote many passages in a garbled form." But the reason for it all is that "they omit the clearest Scriptural passages on faith [the one article of Christianity], select the passages on works, and even distort these. . . . *They teach the law in such a way as to hide the Gospel of Christ*" (286). And because this is the upshot of Roman exegesis — that the Gospel gets hidden and Christ gets buried — Melanchthon cannot say it is accidental. They must be doing it on purpose, making up their exegesis "to evade the Scriptures" (321). Incredible as it sounds, the official leaders of the church "understand neither the forgiveness of sins nor faith nor grace nor righteousness." In short, they do not understand "the main doctrine of Christianity" (2 f), the one article by which the church stands or falls.

In discussing the key to the Scriptures, Melanchthon's favorite term is *Promise*. In his *Loci Communes,* 10 years before, he had stated the definition: *Evangelium est promissio.* This is an important shift from what the word *Gospel* had regularly meant in medieval theology. Of course the term was used, but it was defined differently. It was viewed as *philosophia coelestis,* or the *lex Christi,* or the historical report of Christ's biography. Of course the Gospel is a historical report, but it is more. It contains a compelling assertion about *today* (contemporary history) and not simply about yesterday. And

---

[4] These and all subsequent numbers refer to the numbered paragraphs in Ap IV. Quotations are from the Tappert edition.

even more it is "Promise," because it says something about future history, revealing the potentiality of what is to come — a potentiality that points beyond the "now" and the "here." Viewing the Gospel as a promise moves it away from the "I-it" relationship, as though it were a "thing" — information, rules, reports, even *divine* information, *divine* rules, *divine* reports — and defines it in terms of an "I-Thou" relationship. For whenever I encounter a promise, it is the promissor himself (not an it, but a person) with whom I am actually dealing, and I know it. The promise calls to my attention a present reality, piece of history, about the promissor and also future possibilities with the promissor to which this promise points. There is a parallel on the human level in the promise to marry. Not an it but a thou, a person, is the focal point of the promise. The present tense of the promise signifies his trustworthiness and my confidence in his trustworthiness. Future consequences are the prospect of marriage and a future history with the promissor. And when the future time of marriage comes, that too is sealed with another promise of fidelity which again has the person-to-person focus, the present pledge and confidence in the pledge, and the future prospect of this pledge and confidence lived out.

Melanchthon got the word *Promise* especially from St. Paul and the Epistle to the Hebrews, where the term is used of God and His people under both old and new covenants. St. Paul himself contrasts "Promise" with "Law." In fact it is more explicitly Pauline to speak in terms of Law and Promise than of Law and Gospel, for Paul never explicitly juxtaposes the latter two terms. In any case, for Melanchthon the Reformation understanding of the one chief article of Christianity is called "Promise," and anything in the relations between God and man that is not Promise is "Law." So also anything that the Bible says about God and man must be either Law or Promise — unless there were some third, neutral category of God-man relations, which the Confessions do not allow. So Melanchthon says: "All Scripture should be divided into these two chief doctrines, the law and the promises. In some places it presents the law. In others it presents the promise of Christ." (5)

"Of these two doctrines our opponents select the law" (7) and set up their theology from that. That is the distinctive hermeneutic principle of the Confutation. Theoretically that might be justified, if there were two alternatives in Scripture from which one could choose to concentrate on one and subordinate the other. But Melanchthon's point is that in choosing the Law as the hermeneutical key they do not merely subordinate the Promise, but they bury Him who is the Promise incarnate.

When Melanchthon says, on the other hand, that the Scriptural key for the Lutheran hermeneutics is the Promise, he does not fear that, as with the Law, there will be a corresponding kind of burying. On the contrary, the Scriptural assertions about God's expectations of us are not buried but are brought to full fruition. After I have encountered the Promise, it then becomes possible for me to begin to keep the Law, not only in its second table but also in its first and prior table of "fearing, loving, trusting God."

So a Promise-centered hermeneutics opens up both the legal and the promissive material in Scripture. A Law-centered hermeneutics actually destroys both. Not only does it bury the Promise, but in burying the Promise it makes impossible the keeping of the Law as well. Thereby both words of God are wasted. In Melanchthon's recurrent phrase, they are "in vain."

A legal hermeneutics is not just an intellectual error, an accidental misreading of the Scriptures. Connected with such a hermeneutics, if not in fact the ground of its being, is the fact that "natural man" (any normal sinner) is naturally drawn to such a hermeneutics. "Men naturally trust their own righteousness" (20). "This wicked idea about works has always clung to the world" (206). "We know how repulsive this teaching [the promise] is to the judgment of reason" (230). "This legalistic opinion {opinio legis} clings by nature to the minds of men, and it cannot be driven out unless we are divinely taught." Needed is a turn "from such fleshly opinions to the Word of God" (265 f.). "By nature men judge that God ought to be appeased by works" (393). A legal hermeneutics is therefore not just an intellectual error, but it is ultimately a function of the sinful man. The very fact that it is so automatically attractive to me ought to be the red flag warning me to beware. What Melanchthon is here saying is that the natural man already has a "way of interpreting Scriptures" — and it is a bad one. It must be destroyed and replaced by a hermeneutical key which is as audacious as the Promise itself.

Melanchthon says that the very legal material in the Scriptures already contradicts the hermeneutics of legalism. He notes that "all the Scriptures and the church proclaim that the law cannot be satisfied. The incipient keeping of the law does not please God for its own sake, but for the sake of faith in Christ. Without this, the law always accuses us" *(lex semper accusat,* 166 f.). (Notice the "saintly sins" of which even the best Christian is guilty when the Law accuses him, 167 f.) This leads Melanchthon to posit what he himself calls a "rule . . . [that] interprets all the passages . . . on law and works" (185). The rule is: To all the statements about the Law and works "we must *add"* that the "law cannot be kept without Christ" and that "faith is necessary" (184). There is the audacity of the Lutheran hermeneutics: "adding" things to Scripture. Melanchthon asserts that this is the way Scripture itself treats the Law. "The Scriptures . . . praise works in such a way as not to remove the free promise." (188)

In another place Melanchthon can call for considering "passages in their context" (280). The context he has in mind is not simply the preceding and succeeding passages (although he finds Roman exegesis often guilty here). But the context of Melanchthon's own statement shows that he has in mind the *theological* context, the context finally of the whole redemptive work of God. This notion of the theological context of any Biblical passage leads to his statements about "adding" something to a Bible passage. It seems at first that Melanchthon commits the very same fallacy of addition of which he had accused his opponents, the only difference being in the *content* of his particular addition. He notes that they add the *opinio legis* when treating legal passages and that most often they completely ignore promissive passages (264). Melanchthon himself says, however, that Christ must be added to the total exegesis of a passage if for some reason He is not there originally. When the Confutation gives what we might call a "straight" exegesis of certain legal passages, Melanchthon replies that in preaching (interpreting) the Law there are two things we must always keep in mind: to wit, Christ is needed for anyone to keep the Law, and outward works done without Christ do not please God (256). Then he says, "It is necessary to add the Gospel promise" (257). A bit later, and still on the same subject, he says, "The preaching of the Gospel must be added" (260). When the confuters quote Luke 11:41 ("in garbled form") to show that almsgiving makes a man clean, Melanchthon responds: "Our opponents must be deaf. Over and over we say that the Gospel of Christ must be added to the preaching of the law." (281)

This is one rule of interpretation which Melanchthon says must be maintained by virtue of what the New Testament itself says.

In support he quotes John 15:5 ("Apart from Me you can do nothing") and Heb. 11:6 ("Without faith it is impossible to please God," 372). So in an exegetical situation which without reference to faith in Christ calls for man to do good works and to please God, faith in the righteousness of Christ *must be added* to the Bible passage *because the Bible itself demands it.*

By using this principle Melanchthon is able to take what is supposedly the most embarrassing Bible passage for Lutherans, James 2:24 ("You see that a man is justified by works and not by faith alone"), and show that "this text is more against our opponents than against us." (245)

What is striking about this Lutheran hermeneutics is that it is not first of all based on intellectual principles — like scientific admonitions to be open-minded and unprejudiced, to look at the grammar, syntax, forms of literature, *Weltanschauung* in which the message is couched, etc., but is based on theological principles and convictions, namely, that the ultimate Word of God is Promise and therefore must be present in the written Word.

The counterpart to this theological conviction about the nature and content of what God wants to communicate is the Reformers' constant theological presupposition about the hearer, the listener, the exegete himself, who is on the receiving end of a piece of interpreted Scripture. It is the Reformers' theological conviction that he is either an out-and-out sinner and nothing more, or he is the only other alternative, a sinner-saint, a Christian. Most often Melanchthon has the sinner-saint in mind as the one on the receiving end of his Biblical interpretation. In the practice of exegesis this consideration and evaluation of the man on the receiving end also functions like something of a "hermeneutic rule" in Apology IV. The rule runs somewhat along this line: Only that is a valid interpretation of the written Word which is helpful to the eventual receiver. It does not begin to be helpful until he hears, first, *that* the text is talking about him — better, that God is talking to him about himself — and then hears *what* God is saying to him about himself.

Now one might come to the conclusion that following these principles would lead to a very short-lived study of the Bible. Once a person had learned what the Gospel was, he would have finished. He would know it all, and that would be that. But that is not the case with the actual Christian whom Melanchthon has in mind. This

Christian, though he is God's saint, is still plagued by "saintly" sins (167). So what he needs to have, and what God wants him to receive from the Scriptures, is help on how to *use* Christ. Now that he knows Christ, he needs to learn how to let both the Law and the Promise move into his life — the Law to expose those areas where his idolatry is still thriving, the Promise to have Christ take over those areas and have them function as sectors of redeemed creation and not of the condemned old creation. Christians must be told — and that, as in John 20:31, is the Scriptures' own objective — how faith comes into being, how the Holy Spirit is given, how regeneration takes place, how good works can be done. The purpose is not that they will have the right answer for the great final examination but rather that they can have that answer happening in their own lives now.

Melanchthon's answer to such "how" questions is regularly expressed as "using Christ." "Christ is mediator," he says, but "how will Christ be the mediator if we do not use him as mediator in our justification?" (69). "The Gospel . . . compels us to make use of Christ in justification" (291). "Christ's glory becomes brighter when we teach men to make use of him as mediator and propitiator" (299). That this does not just mean using Christ when we are initially converted or saved is clear from Melanchthon's favored phrase: *Christus manet mediator.* Christ has to *remain* mediator, or else even the Christians would be lost, for the saintly sins cited above are still exposed by the corollary: *Lex semper accusat,* even in Christians. Another frequently repeated notion is that we need to be taught how to use Christ against the wrath of God which threatens our old Adam. And as far as lawkeeping is concerned, the Christian "still" needs Christ's help "to keep the law" (299). One of the most critical assertions by Melanchthon against Roman exegesis is that "they do not teach us to use Christ as the mediator." (313)

Because the Roman hermeneutics allows men to bypass Jesus Christ, yes, even bury Him, it comes as no surprise that Melanchthon sees the same hermeneutic principles operating in Roman exegesis which had operated in first-century Pharisaic Judaism. Judaism was the first to bypass Jesus Christ and also to bury Him. On one occasion Melanchthon says: "This is what we condemn in our opponents' position, that by interpreting such passages of the Scriptures in . . . a Jewish manner they eliminate from them the righteousness of faith and Christ, the mediator" (376). Or in a moment of righteous wrath: "Cursed be our opponents, those Pharisees, who interpret the law in such a way that . . . [men have] access to the Father . . . without Christ, the mediator" (269). It was surely this parallel between their conflict with Rome and Jesus' own conflict with Pharisaic Judaism that added weight to the Reformers' conviction that their hermeneutics was valid. A classical document which consciously observes this parallelism in action is Luther's larger commentary on Galatians (1535). The premise here is that Luther's hermeneutics is Paul's heremeneutics, yes, is Christ's own hermeneutics.

One last observation might still be drawn from Apology IV. Melanchthon is conscious that he is working with an interpretation of Scripture different from the one his opponents employ. But is his interpretation really so distinctively new? It is not, according to Melanchthon himself. Together with Luther he asserts that this hermeneutics was Jesus' own as He battled with Judaism, and Paul's own, and John's (5:39), and that of the author of Hebrews, et al.; and he adds that it was also the working method of interpretation among the fathers of the church and among the common Christians who make up the span from the first to the 16th century. He cites numerous church fathers to this effect.

But this is not the clinching argument which convinces Melanchthon that the Reformers' hermeneutics is valid, namely the mere fact that it has been in practice, at least in some places, throughout the history of the church. What makes this hermeneutics convincingly valid is that it serves the worship of that Christ whom the Quasimodogeniti Gospel reminds us is "my Lord and my God." The greatest worship of Christ is to use Him and His benefits for the purpose God intended — in the words of the same Gospel lection, "that you might have life in His name."

Perhaps there are other operating procedures for exegesis in our time which are not identical with those the Reformers utilize. There are no *a priori* reasons why one could not use the tools of source criticism and *Formgeschichte* and still be interpreting the Scriptures in keeping with these Lutheran hermeneutic principles. But any hermeneutics, however critical or simple or orthodox, if it commits the fallacy which Melanchthon saw committed by the Confutation of his day, will have to be rejected, not because Luther says so nor even because the Confessions say so, but because it buries Christ. Conversely, the only reason there is a Christian church engaged in interpreting the Scriptures at all is that Christ is not buried but "is arisen" — "that we might have life in His name."

"... the act of God climaxing in Christ Jesus on the Cross is proclaimed as an act in time past now applied to action in time present."

CHAPTER 7

The Preacher
and the Proclamation

Some Architectural Reflections on Gaps and Bridges

JOHN H. ELLIOTT

"Preaching is God's Word in Christ to people." This homiletical axiom was formulated by the distinguished sexagenarian to whose honor this collection of essays is dedicated. "This principle," Caemmerer goes on to explain, "is in the forefront of contemporary Christian thought because of fresh interest in Biblical studies, concern for the theology of the church, and new insight into the meaning of the Word of God." [1] From this vantage point the nexus between preaching and exegesis or Biblical study appears self-evident and unassailable. To judge from the concerns expressed in other quarters, however, this opinion does not appear to be unanimous. For across the country and across the sea and throughout the various denominations theologians, clergy, and laymen are noting with increasing alarm a distance, a gap, which has been developing between exegetical theology and not only the theologizing of the parish pastor but also the other disciplines of the theological curriculum as well. In a stimulating article which attempts to analyze the present state of this problem, the New Testament scholar Robert W. Funk objects that an exclusive emphasis upon the *"scientific* and *scholarly* aspect of exegetical research has led to an incestuous scholarly tradition that has lost touch, by and large, with the theological and ecclesiastical situation." [2]

[1] Richard R. Caemmerer, *Preaching for the Church* (St. Louis: Concordia Publishing House, 1959), p. xi.
[2] "Creating an Opening: Biblical Criticism and the Theological Curriculum," *Interpretation* XVIII (October 1964), 387—406, esp. 387.

It is certainly true that new discoveries of material, new methods of analysis, and new approaches to the hermeneutical question of understanding have brought about a *specialization* within exegetical theology. This "new look" of exegesis in many aspects is part of the common product of the new scientific age. And Funk points out effectively that this progress, or — more neutrally speaking, if you will — this change, involves banes as well as blessings. This development and specialization inward has not favored a conversation outward, a dialog with the other theological disciplines. Instead, specialization has led to isolation — not only within the exegetical area but among the areas of church history, systematics, and practical theology as well. This isolation is particularly evident at theological seminaries, where each department employs a jargon peculiar to its own area and attempts carefully to define its own specific task over against the other departments. In the process, the questions raised by students which emerge from the total context of theological experience and concern are treated by each department in only restrictive fashion. Such a precise definition of the peculiar concerns of exegetical, historical, systematic, and practical theology are, of course, essential to the proper functioning of the curriculum. The imminent danger of this process, which too often becomes evident reality, however, is that the seminarian seldom learns how to put all the pieces of his jigsaw puzzle together. Eventually he feels that he too is left only with the choice of specializing in one area or, in utter despair, of forsaking all concern whatsoever with such "pigeon-hole theologizing." Later on in his "practical" ministry he ends up repelling the various theologizing attempts of the "specialists" as unhelpful, irrelevant, and perhaps even destructive.

This growing gap between scientific Biblical study and pastoral activity has been seen on a horizon even broader than the theological curriculum and the activity of one particular American church body. One of the leading critics of the "What's wrong with American religion?" school, Dr. Martin E. Marty of Chicago, in his study *The New Shape of American Religion*[3] points out that one of the chief causes of malfunction in American religion is that religion is no more than an attitude, an American way of life, whose moorings in a sound Biblical theology have long been severed. If this man-centered and ultimately self-destructive view of religion is to be rectified, insists

[3] New York: Harper and Brothers, 1958, esp. pp. 83, 111.

Marty, then attention will have to be given to a theology whose shape is determined rather by the prophetic voice issuing from careful Biblical exegesis than by the "metaphysical sanctions" and "ceremonial reinforcements" of a democratic Pan-Protestantism.

Within the scope of this study it would be impossible, obviously, to consider all the ramifications of the problems stressed by these critics. Rather here we shall restrict our discussion to the relationship between exegetical and practical theology. That is, we shall reflect upon some basic methodological considerations concerning the task of exegesis (used here as a comprehensive designation for the analysis and exposition of the Sacred Scriptures) and the task of preaching (the communication and application of this divine Word to all the people of the present day, both within and without the church).

Three observations might commend such a limitation of scope. (1) There is an obvious integral connection between exegesis and preaching. Even those parish pastors who seem to find little or no time for Biblical study or those theological "specialists" who appear to exegize merely for the sake of exegizing would hardly disagree with this point — at least in principle. (2) This relationship removes the issue from the danger of being a merely academic or curricular concern. For the relationship between exegesis and preaching, between exposition and application, is one which is at the heart of the tensions not only within the seminary but also between the seminary and the "field," that is, the congregations whom the seminarians are being trained to serve. This also involves the tension within the individual pastor, a tension caused by the demand that he be both exegete and preacher. (3) Consideration of this particular topic would be a most appropriate manner in which a former student might acknowledge his debt of gratitude to and recognize the central concern of the man whom he is privileged to call his teacher and father in God.

In this consideration of the relationship between exegesis and preaching an attempt will be made to define clearly the gaps which separate exegesis from preaching, thus showing how this question is but part of the larger problem cited above. Second, at the hand of Biblical texts suggestions will be made toward the possible bridging of those gaps. Third and finally, a few questions concerning the "Caemmererian approach" will be raised.

This study does not presume to offer new insights. Its purpose, rather, is to recall and reemphasize some of the basic principles concerning the purpose and function of both the exegete and the preacher.

The aim of such a review would be the clarification of the relationship between these two tasks and of the contribution which an accurate execution of the former can and should make toward a successful completion of the latter.

Between exegesis and preaching today there is a tension. This tension is a product of the larger problem facing modern theology as presented above. While to some degree tension is part of the general dialectic process of life, and particularly of theology, it is an unhealthy relation which is meant here, an unhealthy tension which manifests itself in the kinds of attitudes which the preacher takes over against the exegetical task.

First there is the "practical" preacher who considers exegesis too specialized, too academic, and too scientific to have any bearing on the "low level" problems and the "simple speaking of the simple Word of God" in which he is engaged. He readily admits that he is no theologian. Though he once appreciated vaguely the significance of an aorist indicative and a *hithpael,* this appreciation has been worn thin by the erosive forces of competing interests and the suspicion that exegesis would not contribute to or change his sermons anyway.

Some preachers continue to bolster these reflections (mostly subconscious) with the thought that reading the text in translation (English, German, or some other contemporary idiom) is certainly sufficient and that the text, on the whole, will be clear enough. After all, is not this a key item in a Lutheran conception of Scripture, the perspicuity of the Word of God? For such men exegesis is thus unnecessary for the preparation of preaching.

On the other hand, there are many pastors and not a few theologians who see no basic difference between exegesis and preaching. For are not both activities concerned with the same thing: interpreting the Word of God? The ultimate result of this attitude is that one of the two tasks, usually exegesis, is then considered superfluous. A good exegete, it is said, is a priori a good preacher; and a good preacher is a posteriori a good exegete. If the former opinion is more typical of the European assumption, the latter certainly applies to the popular American conception. Men holding this opinion customarily introduce the sermon text with words such as "What St. Paul (or St. Luke) is saying to *us* this morning is . . ." thus implying that Paul or Luke had in mind not only their own contemporaries but also 20th-century Americans. Or they will occasionally introduce Greek or Hebrew words into the sermon, quote the opinion of some respect-able commentator, or fill up the sermon with lengthy reviews of the history of the Israelites or the childhood of Jesus. According to this attitude exegesis and preaching are one and the same thing.

A third group of preachers would constitute those who, like theo-logical versions of Kant, recognize that "without believing theology all scientific theology is empty, and without scientific theology all believing theology is blind." They agree that exegesis is more than pious meditation on a text. They would like to make careful exegeti-cal analysis a part of every sermon preparation, but they are not quite sure how to go about it. Perhaps they fear that they have lost their command of Hebrew and Greek. Or perhaps they are uncertain about the precise procedure to follow. Whatever the case might be, they are not now engaging in the exegetical task because they do not know how.

Common to all three attitudes is an unclarity concerning the relationship between exegesis and preaching. In the first instance exegesis is thought to be unnecessary for preaching; in the second instance exegesis is considered identical with preaching; and in the third case exegesis is omitted because the preacher is uncertain about what the exegetical task really is.

For the sake of comprehensiveness a fourth attitude might be mentioned — that attitude prevalent among those relatively few the-ologians who consider exegesis to be only a historical discipline whose aim is exclusively the illumination of a literary product of the past. This view, which fails to see exegesis as the prelude to proclamation, fortunately is quite rare and is not to be identified promiscuously with all form critics or historical critics who emphasize exegesis' concern with the historical.

Thus in order to meet this problem of unclarity in all of its manifestations it would seem profitable at this point to attempt a defi-nition as precisely and briefly as possible of both the homiletical and the exegetical tasks. On the basis of these definitions we shall then be prepared to discuss the precise relationship between the two activi-ties.

"Preaching," to return to our aforementioned homiletical axiom, "is God's Word in Christ to people." There is a polarity to the homiletical task, a movement about two foci: the Word of God and people. The task of the preacher, in simplest terms, is to relate and apply the former to the latter. In order to do this he must know both poles equally well. On the one hand, the preacher must know his audience, its general psychological and sociological structure, its specific interests and problems, and the entire cultural context — education, arts, music, politics, economics, and so forth — which makes up its life situation. On the other hand, he must also know God's Word, the Word of punishment and pardon, wrath and mercy, destruction and deliverance, as it was directed to the old and the new creations, Israel and the church. And then in his preaching he embarks upon the task of correlation, relating this *ephapax* Word of God addressed to historical situations of a past age to a new contemporary situation. Preaching, therefore, has as its prerequisites careful analyses of both the contemporary audience and the divine Word of old.

But, it might be questioned, is such a correlation even possible? Are there not insurmountable gaps between this present situation and that of old? The factors of the canon and the normative character of the Scriptures, though pertinent to this subject, are not implied here. For a basic presupposition of the Lutheran exegete is that the divine Word is the source, foundation, and norm for subsequent formulations of or discussion about the Word.[4] Rather by "gaps" are meant those factors which separate the preacher of the 20th century from the Word which he would preach. We mention only five of the basic ones: the gap of language, the gap of culture, the gap of geography, the gap of history, and the gap of theology/anthropology (*Weltanschauung, Gottesanschauung,* and *Selbstanschauung*).

The Sacred Scriptures are the written products of language, a language which is foreign to a modern preacher's own people and age: Hebrew, Aramaic, and Greek. This means that the Scriptures are *not* immediately comprehendable by anyone who would merely seek their "simple sense" — unless he can sight-read Hebrew, Aramaic, and/or Greek. This language gap thus represents one of the hindrances to an accurate understanding of the Scriptures. In order that these writings become understandable — at least linguistically and grammatically — and communicable, they must be translated into

    [4] Cf. FC SD, *De compendiaria doctrinae forma, fundamento, norma atque regula,* 3. English translation in *The Book of Concord: The Confessions of the Evangelical Lutheran Church,* trans. and ed. Theodore G. Tappert in collaboration with Jaroslav Pelikan, Robert H. Fischer, and Arthur C. Piepkorn (Philadalphia: Muhlenberg [Fortress] Press, 1959), pp. 503—504.

the contemporary idiom. Yet as a contemporary German exegete, Ernst Fuchs, has recognized, "every translation is a tour de force."[5] These writings have been composed in a thought world and milieu that is different from today's. Whether a literal translation or a paraphrase is attempted, the original unity of language and spirit, the original *Lebensgefühl,* is replaced and thus lost. *That* we must translate is obvious and inevitable. Obvious and inevitable also, however, is the fact that no translation is ever an exact one. The translator never "simply" translates. Every translation is also an interpretation. Certainly for sermon preparation the use of a modern version of the Bible is better than no use of the Bible at all. Nevertheless, the preacher must be aware that, whatever his choice of "ponies" might be, such a translation is always second-rate and at best a "puzzling reflection," always more or less but never exactly the same as the original text being translated.

This language gap is but a part of a larger cultural gap. The Sacred Scriptures are products of their own Palestinean and Judaeo-Hellenic culture. The social customs peculiar to this setting find few remnants in this atomic age. Even the state of Nevada requires more substantial reasons for divorce than did the Jewish society of the first century A. D. As for the children who grow up on the pavements and in the alleys of downtown New York, Chicago, or San Francisco, they might never in their lives see a real pig or ever be able to make much sense of the agricultural parable of the sower and the seed.

Moreover, a geographical gap is evident in the books which reflect the distant geography of the Fertile Crescent and the Mediterranean world. Israel's religious experience and theological reflection were intimately bound to the hot devastating winds from the south, the monsters of the Mediterranean deep, and the mountaintop abodes of the gods. The whole world of the primitive church was that of the Mediterranean region. To call a less than genteel member of society a "corinthian" was far worse than to label him "southern white trash" or a "Bronx bum."

The factor of history also separates the preacher from his text. These writings are the products of a dim and distant past. More than 1,700 years separate the composition of the first and last books of the Bible, and almost 2,000 years more separate the present-day reader from even the most recent of these documents. In the meantime all

---

[5] *Hermeneutik* (Bad Canstatt, 1954), pp. 103 f.

the original documents have been lost or destroyed. All that the church today possesses are copies and copies of copies ad infinitum — copies which have been subject to all the ravages of time, nature, and the human fallibilities of inaccurate and overzealous scribes and editors.

Finally, the Scriptures sometimes speak of God, the gods, and man in ways strange and alien to contemporary man: the Genesis picture of a 3-story universe, the gods who live in valleys and on mountain peaks, the man whose bowels are the seat of his compassion.

These factors, which reflect the very nature of the Scriptures, constitute gaps which separate the preacher and his historical situation from the writings which he would make the basis of his proclamation. They represent, in effect, hindrances to present-day understanding.

It may be suggested, for instance, that no one would claim a Biblical text such as the Holy Gospel for the Second Sunday in Advent (Luke 21:25-36) to be immediately and thoroughly comprehensible. What is the nature of these forthcoming "signs in sun and moon and stars," these apocalyptic images of the Last Day to which Jesus here refers? When and how shall earth-dwellers of the end time faint with fear and nations be distressed and perplexed at the "roaring of the sea and the waves"? Precisely how are these to be understood as manifestations of the coming of the Son of Man? It has been proposed with a reasonable amount of substantiation that Luke understood these words of Jesus in connection with the destruction of Jerusalem in A. D. 70. Is this what Jesus Himself had in mind? Furthermore, the subsequent history of the church is dotted with chiliastic movements and bands of doomsday enthusiasts who searched the heavens and contemporary events for such signs in their own day and found them forecasting the end of the world in the second century, the 16th, 18th, and at the thresholds of both World Wars. How does the one holy catholic church understand these words today? Certainly one acquainted with the apocalyptic imagery of the early centuries and its import searches far and wide indeed for an understanding and appreciation of the eschatological impact of this Advent message — to say nothing of the ability to communicate it!

And even these factors do not exhaust the list of difficulties separating the preacher from his text. For even assuming that the divine Word once addressed to one historical situation can be addressed to another historical situation centuries later, the question arises *how* this can be done. What is the method? What are the criteria? Furthermore, it should be recognized that these writings now used as "texts" were never intended for that purpose. Isaiah and Jeremiah, Matthew and Paul did not write in order to supply the church with "sermon texts." Rather these literary products were meant to be sermons themselves! Thus the modern preacher, when basing his sermon on a Biblical text, is in effect preaching a new sermon on an old sermon. And the question must at least be raised as to whether such a procedure of turning a sermon into a text allows the present church to remain faithful to the original design of these documents.

All these questions and all these gaps touch a common problem — the problem of understanding. What we have enumerated are hindrances to an accurate comprehension of the original intent and purpose of the writings which form the norm for all the church's theology and proclamation. This means that if the preacher is accurately and faithfully to apply the Word of God to his people, then he must not only *recognize* that there are serious hindrances to this goal but also find a *way of overcoming* them. The means open to him — the only means which the church catholic in opposition to all attempts on the part of the *Schwaermer* and the mystics, has consistently espoused — is that of exegetical investigation. For this is the purpose of exegesis: to overcome the hindrances to understanding by building bridges to span the gaps. Once the preacher is prepared to acknowledge this need of bridge building, then the next step is an obvious one: to define precisely what are the components of the exegetical bridge.

So far we have been employing the term *exegesis* as a collective designation for the various elements of the task of interpretation. It would be more proper, however, to speak of three areas of this process of interpretation: hermeneutics, exegesis proper, and isagogics.

Hermeneutics is the most comprehensive of these terms and deals with the question of understanding in all of its ramifications. Though in former centuries the term was used in connection with the interpretation of Holy Scripture, in more recent time, particularly since the work of Schleiermacher, Dilthey, and Heidegger, hermeneu-

tics has been employed in a more extended sense. Thus Gerhard
Ebeling, in his essay "The Word of God and Hermeneutics" [6] points
out that hermeneutics has come to be used in other sciences that deal
with the problem of understanding, such as psychology. In philosophy
it takes the place of classical epistemological theory and becomes the
essence of fundamental ontology. Even in connection with theology
the word has been extended in meaning so that Fuchs, for instance,
speaks of hermeneutics as *Sprachlehre des Glaubens,* the "grammar
of faith."

It would be beyond the purpose of this study, however, either
to trace the development of this extension of meaning or to defend
a more narrow sense. Certainly the latter is by no means rejected
by Ebeling, Fuchs, and others, once the hermeneutical question of
understanding has been seen in its broader context. Therefore with
hermeneutics we are talking about the principles, the guidelines, for
an accurate understanding of the Holy Scriptures. This involves certain presuppositions concerning not only the nature of that which
is to be interpreted, that is, the Bible, but also regarding the manner
in which such interpretation is to be executed. A basic presupposition
of most Christian expositors, for instance, is that the Bible is the Word
of God. This is a conviction of faith even in the case of Paul's words
to Timothy, "All Scripture . . ." Only as the Spirit of God leads to
faith does any expositor believe that the Bible is the Word of God.
This position determines what Rudolf Bultmann has called the
Woraufhin der Befragung, the direction of concern in the Book to
be analyzed. The Christian exegete is concerned about this sacred
Book because he believes that the divine Word heard here is a Word
for every people of every age.

Though it might seem superfluous to some, let it be stated
explicitly that form critics and historical critics such as Bultmann,
Fuchs, and others are done a grave injustice when they are accused
of a desire to "demythologize away the Word of God." Rather their
intention is, by way of careful and painstaking analysis, to discover
precisely what that Word really is. "The Word of God," says Bultmann, is that which "confronts me with His mercy and grace. . . .
It is not a possession secured in knowledge, but an address which

---

[6] *Word and Faith,* trans. James W. Leitch (Philadelphia, 1963), pp. 305—
32, esp. pp. 314 ff. In 1960 Ebeling's essay, originally published in *Zeitschrift für
Theologie und Kirche,* LVI (1959), 224—51, was collected in *Wort und Glaube.*

encounters us again and again." [7] The question is not one of attitude but rather one of *method,* and here it may well be that we are compelled to part company. The hermeneutical question, therefore, is the question concerning the Word of God and how that Word became and becomes an event, both in the past and in the present.[8]

The science of hermeneutics, therefore, attempts to devise a set of guidelines for interpretation and understanding, which guidelines themselves are determined by the very nature of the object to be understood, the Holy Scriptures. Thus hermeneutics emphasizes the necessity of philological, literary, and historical criticism, which are all attempts to distinguish, evaluate (using "criticism" in its properly neutral and scientific sense), and do justice to the linguistic, literary, and historical character of the Bible. All of these subdisciplines are products of the exegetical insights of Luther, Calvin, and other Reformation fathers who appreciated and emphasized the one literal-historical sense of Scripture, the necessity of philological and historical analysis, and the unity of Spirit and language. Likewise hermeneutics calls attention to the unity of the Testaments, the context of the total Scriptures, and the *viva vox evangelii.* It is within the context of this concept of the Scriptures as the Word of God and according to the principles of interpretation deriving from these Scriptures that the task of exegesis proper is carried out.

In short, hermeneutics in its broadest sense is a science concerned with the issue of understanding and meaning. The particular text or canonized group of texts with which this science deals, known as Holy Scripture, is the object of its examination because the transmitter of these texts, the church, considers them to contain a meaning not only for the past but also for every new and subsequent present. The hermeneutical question thus arises from a desire, on the one hand, of every new generation to understand these texts and appropriate their meaning for itself; and, on the other, from the inability to do so directly and immediately because of certain gaps separating the present from the past, the meaning from him who would understand.

In order to bridge these gaps certain disciplines within the hermeneutical task become necessary. The most inclusive of these sub-

---

[7] "Rudolf Bultmann: Bultmann Replies to His Critics," *Kerygma and Myth,* ed. H. W. Bartsch and trans. R. H. Fuller from *Kerygma und Mythus,* I (London, 1957), 207.

[8] Cf. Ebeling, pp. 313 ff.

sidiary disciplines is known as exegesis. A second such discipline, interrelated with the first, is isagogics.

Exegesis "leads out" the meaning of the text. The goal of the exegete is to determine with all the philological and historical tools and skills at his disposal as accurately as possible what a particular text (in our case Biblical text) *meant* for its particular author and its particular addressees. Lest the peculiar task of exegesis be mistaken, the stress on the verb of past tense, *meant,* dare not be overlooked.

New Testament scholar Krister Stendahl of Harvard University, in a careful description of the task of Biblical theology,[9] accurately insists on a distinction by Biblical theologians between the past and the present meanings of a text, between what the text *meant* when it was first written and what it *means* today. Whereas hermeneutics is characterized by the tension of being concerned for both questions, exegesis is interested exclusively in the first: What did the text mean in its original peculiar historical context? Exegesis has no business inquiring what meaning that same text might or might not have today. To be sure, the question is essential and therefore by all means legitimate. The question of a text's *present* meaning, however, is the concern not of the exegete but of the preacher. The degree of accuracy with which exegete and preacher each executes his respective task will be measured by the awareness each one has of the limitations as well as the requirements of his own discipline.

An exegete who meditates on the significance of the text for himself and his generation instead of asking what it meant for its own generation, who substitutes application for analysis by introducing his would-be exegetical observations with "What Paul is saying to *us* is . . ." or who reads into the Gospel of John the ontological concerns of an existentialist philosophy, has failed to be faithful to the purely descriptive nature of the exegetical task. He is as deserving of censure as the preacher at the other extreme who burdens his communication of the Good News with Greek verbs and Hebrew constructs and belabors his much-too-patient and probably stupefied audience with archaeological data from the latest Ta'anach dig or geographical niceties regarding the Mount of Olives. Both description and application have their necessary and undisputed place in theology. The mark of superior exegetes and preachers, however, is that they know what that place is.

9 "Biblical Theology, Contemporary," *Interpreter's Dictionary of the Bible,* ed. G. A. Buttrick (New York/Nashville: Abingdon Press, 1962), I, 418—32.

The task of exegesis is an analytic and descriptive one. Basically, the old synonym for exegesis serves as well as any to characterize its function: *expositio*.[10] The exegete can be compared to a heart surgeon who reaches the object of his concern by making an incision into the flesh surrounding the heart, exploring the region, and finally exposing that section of the heart to be treated. In order to determine the heart of his text, its meaning, the exegete too must first expose all the elements by which that meaning is maintained, manifested, and communicated: the text's structure and form, its literary genre, its historical context, the geographical, cultural, and other *realia* employed therein, and the purpose of the literary whole of which it forms a part.

To return to our example of the text from the Second Sunday in Advent (Luke 21:25-36), the exegete seeks to determine the significance of this pericope within the third gospel and the first-century church. How did Luke and his contemporaries understand these words about the signs of the end? What do these images signify and what is their possible origin? What is the source of this tradition containing Jesus' description of the Son of Man's coming and how did Luke employ it? What role did this conception of the Last Day play within the apocalyptic and eschatological views of history in the first Christian century and what role within the message of Luke? Such an attempt to question the text, to expose the text so that it might yield its meaning, is an attempt to be as critical with the text as possible. The word "critical" does not have the exclusively negative connotations of its popular usage. "Criticism" by definition does not denote primarily a negative evaluation but implies in its original Greek sense the activity of "dividing, distinguishing, and differentiating," steps which are at the basis of true science. Thus, according to *Webster's Seventh New Collegiate Dictionary,* criticism is "the art of evaluating or analyzing with knowledge and propriety."

The various activities of exegesis are thus known as textual criticism, literary criticism, form criticism, redaction criticism, tradition criticism, and finally a *Sachkritik,* a criticism of the content itself, in connection with all the information available concerning the historical and cultural milieu, thought world, and religious environment in which this text was born. Each of these further subdisciplines of

---

[10] It is unnecessary here to discuss the various nuances of and possible differentiations between exposition, clarification, interpretation, and related synonyms so long as the basic stress on the descriptive nature of the task is borne in mind.

exegesis is a product of the recognition of many particular factors and situations accompanying and underlying the composition of the Biblical documents. Each particular discipline is an attempt to recognize and deal with specific literary and historical characteristics of the structure, form, and content of the Biblical text. From the concerns for such characteristics exegesis has received its designation as essentially philological-historical criticism.

Exegesis is to be conceived as involving a process of asking and answering. The product of exegesis assumes the form of an answer to certain questions posed by both the exegete and the text. The question involved here is this: What is the text saying, what is its meaning? These are questions posed to the text, or more specifically, to the author of the text, and questions posed indirectly by the text. Again we have the polarity of questioner and text and the distance between these two — all characteristic of the hermeneutical problem.[11] Exegesis is possible and necessary only where these questions exist, and such questions exist only where the distance between questioner and text has become obvious. The questions which the exegete poses are queries determined both by the interests of the community of which the exegete is a member, the church of his own era, and by the nature of the text or collection of texts in which he is interested. In his task of philological-historical criticism the exegete not only seeks answers to his questions but is also prepared to let the questions of the text, more specifically the questions of God's Word in the text, revise and possibly reject his questions.

For above all, the Biblical exegete, with all his questions and concerns, is not merely dependent on the text but subject to it. Hence his asking and his critical evaluation might properly be called a careful and subordinate listening.[12] If hermeneutics can be understood, in the words of Martin H. Franzmann, as the "laws of good listening," then exegesis might be described as "listening according to these 'laws' . . . in a highly conscious, disciplined, and systematic way."[13]

11 Claus Westermann discusses in more extended scope this question-and-answer character of exegesis in his article "Was ist eine exegetische Aussage?" *Zeitschrift für Theologie und Kirche,* LIX (1962), 1—15.

12 Cf. both Ernst Fuchs, "Was wird in der Exegese des Neuen Testaments interpretiert?" *Zur Frage nach dem historischen Jesus* (Tübingen, J. C. B. Mohr, 1960), pp. 280—303, and Martin H. Franzmann, "Hear Ye Him: Training the Pastor in the Holy Scriptures," *Toward a More Excellent Ministry,* ed. Richard R. Caemmerer and Alfred O. Fuerbringer (St. Louis, Concordia Publishing House, 1964), pp. 81—90.

13 Franzmann, p. 82

This ability to listen to the text and not to speak before the text has spoken constitutes the difference between exegesis and eisegesis.

Still popular in some circles today are such questionable activities as opening the Bible at random and selecting a Bible verse for one's daily *Lebensweg* or rejecting all disciplined analysis of the Bible as an attempt to sit above the Scriptures and in judgment upon them. Such conceptions of God's Word fail to take seriously its historical orientation as a particular word for a particular situation. They not only disparage exegesis; they consider it superfluous. Obviously by "listening" such miscomprehensions are not implied. To listen to a text as a word of God is rather to acknowledge all one's questions and answers as subordinate to the text — judged by the text as valid or invalid. It means recognizing the text as the boundary and limitation of one's questions and answers. This means that the exegete may say only as much as his text says and no more, while at the same time saying all that his text says and no less. As the act of listening determines the nature and degree of one's exegesis, it likewise reminds the exegete-hearer that there are others who would also hear and that his task is but the preliminary step to the preacher's proclamation.

Before the analytic and descriptive attempts of the exegete are employed by the preacher in his organization of a Biblical proclamation for the church of today, one final discipline of the analytic process should be mentioned. Of all the steps of the interpretive task it is possibly this one which more than any other makes the questioner aware of his distance from the text. This is the discipline of isagogics.

Isagogics is that branch of Biblical science which attempts to recognize adequately and pay full tribute to the Biblical documents as documents of particular historical situations of the past. The discipline of isagogics recognizes that each of the documents of both Old and New Testaments is a specific composition of a specific author or authors for a specific audience or audiences at a specific time and in a specific place and addressing a specific situation with a specific message. In dealing with questions of authorship, addressees, time and place of composition, and, most important, occasion and purpose of each of the Biblical documents, isagogics *introduces* the exegete to the major factors which caused, accompanied, and surrounded the composition of each document of Holy Scripture. This is isagogics in the more particular sense of the traditional "special isagogics."

In more general scope isagogics also involves the history of the development of the canon and of the transmission of the Biblical text.
Isagogics involves the *historical* factors in which the sacred writings
were composed, collected, and transmitted. Thus Feine-Behm-Küm-
mel point out that the science of isagogics or "introduction" *(Einleitung)* is "a strictly historical discipline which through the clarification of the historical circumstances prevailing at the origin of the
individual writings provides interpretation with the necessary presuppositions for the understanding of the writings in their historical
individuality; and through the investigation of the development and
preservation of the collection this science provides a sure historical
basis for [treating] the question concerning the doctrinal content
of the New Testament." [14]

The main tool, therefore, of isagogics is that of historical criticism. Of the historical factors subjected to investigation, some are
more important than others. Though scholars of previous generations,
both critical and noncritical, stressed excessively the question of
authorship, for instance, expending much effort either denying or
affirming traditional views, in more recent times it has become clear
that the matter of authorship is of less importance than that of addressees and that the factors of the occasion and purpose of a writing
are most crucial of all. Whether St. Paul, for instance, wrote Philippians is of much less significance than a knowledge of the precise
character of the Christian community at Philippi. Also important are
the factors which gave rise to this letter and what the author intended
to accomplish thereby. For here we are dealing with the Christian
proclamation of the Gospel in concrete situations.

Isagogics aids exegesis in providing the historical context in
which each particular text of every document is to be understood and
interpreted. Of course, the relation between the two tasks is also
circular. For isagogics not only serves but is also served by exegesis,
examining and combining expositions of individual texts in order
to devise a picture of the whole literary product. In this manner
exegetical and isagogical conclusions are interdependent and open-
ended, always subject to correction and revision on the basis of new
evidence. Despite their necessarily tentative character, however, they
provide the basis for a confrontation with the single historical-literal

---

[14] Paul Feine and Johannes Behm, *Einleitung in das Neue Testament,* 12th,
fully rev. ed. Werner Georg Kümmel (Heidelberg, Quelle und Meyer, 1963), p. 5.

sense of Scripture. To overlook or to ignore this point is to be igno-
rant of a fundamental hermeneutical insight of the Reformer Martin
Luther, that the *sensus Scripturae unus est.*

Equally significant among the contributions of exegesis and
its handmaiden isagogics is the manner in which they demonstrate
that the Word of God is first a word addressed to a particular historical situation. It is a divine Word rooted in specific historical
events, spoken by specific men of past time, and addressed to specific
problems of specific audiences also of the past. Form criticism in
particular has called attention to the preaching character of both
Old and New Testament writings from the prophets to the author
of Deuteronomy, from Paul to the four evangelists. Furthermore,
exegesis and isagogics have shown how messages once directed to
one audience were subsequently reinterpreted and addressed to different people in new and different circumstances. The words and events
involving the promises to the patriarchs, the exodus, the giving of
the Law on Mount Sinai, and the words and deeds of Jesus of Nazareth, the preaching of Peter, and the missionizing of Paul — have
undergone some reinterpretation and reapplication at the hands of
later prophets, evangelists, apostles, and seers.

Both exegete and preacher are concerned with and involved
in the hermeneutical issue of understanding. For this is the goal
of both: to understand the meaning of the text so that the believer
in turn might understand God's saving Word to be a Word not for
one age alone but for every age, including the one of which he is
a part, to the end that all men might understand themselves and their
role in the will of God. The specific orientation and the goals of
each discipline, however, vary.

Again the conclusions as well as the posture of the exegete indicate that subjecting the text to historical-critical inquiry is only part
of the task. The text is to be interpreted and applied. This review
of the nature of the task of exegesis in both its broader and more
particular concerns has shown that not only are there differences
between the activities of exposing what the text once meant and proclaiming what it now means, but that both the preacher and the
exegete function capably when each is faithful to his particular discipline and aware of its limitations; without an awareness of the inter-
relatedness of the two neither the exegete nor the preacher would
be faithful to the text and the meaning which he would explore. The

orientation of the exegete is backward, concerned with the past. The
direction of the preacher is forward, facing the present and the future.
The exegete is primarily concerned with what a text meant for its
original author and audience. The preacher is primarily interested
in what a text means for himself and his contemporaries in their
present historical situation. The exegetical task is analytic and descriptive, dealing with words and events which have already taken place.
The homiletical task is synthetic and constructive, spanning both past
and present and creating a new message with a renewed interpretation.
The exegete would know what the character of the Word was then
pro eis, pro eo. The preacher would say what the Word is now; he
would, in brief, make the written Word become a living Word once
again, a Word *pro nobis* and *pro me.*

Exegesis is a discipline of asking, hearing, and listening to what
was said once in the past. Preaching is a discipline of speaking, telling,
and communicating what must be said now in the present. The difference, finally, may be seen as a matter of prepositions. To exegize is
to *ex*pose and lead out the meaning of the text. To preach is to *ap*ply
and *ad*dress that meaning to new people. For those with a systematic
bent *expositio* and *applicatio* might be compared to the two natures
of Christ: In order for the characteristics of each to be accurately
appreciated, the two dare never be separated or confused.

"It is always easier," Rudolf Bultmann has aptly observed, "to
adorn the tombs of the prophets of the past than it is to remain true
to them in the matter with which they themselves were concerned." [15]
If exegesis indeed is not an adornment of the tombs of prophets and
apostles but rather a description of the living and life-related character of their proclamation to their own generations, then exegesis'
final service and ultimate goal is that it enable this divine Word
spoken once in the past to become a living and life-related Word,
a real communication, once again. Thus the exegete will remain
true to the matter with which the proclaimers of old were themselves
concerned. Let us consider therefore a number of Biblical texts, whose
brief analysis might illustrate just how hermeneutics, exegesis, and
isagogics may serve the preacher in the final task of proclaiming the
Word anew.

One of the key issues in the contemporary discussion of Biblical

[15] Rudolf Bultmann, "On Behalf of Christian Freedom," *Existence and
Faith: Shorter Writings of Rudolf Bultmann,* trans. S. M. Ogden (New York:
Meridian Books, 1960), p. 247.

hermeneutics is the question of the relationship between Old and New Testaments, the problem of continuity between Israel and the church. One of the many texts which relate directly to this question is one which reveals the manner in which the Old Testament was cited and interpreted by the first authors of the church — Matt. 2:13-15, the opening verses of the Holy Gospel for the Sunday after New Year. This passage figures significantly in the opening section of the Gospel of Matthew (1:1—4:16) as citing one of the five Old Testament passages which the author has introduced with a stereotype formula as having been "fulfilled" (*{epi}pleroun*). These particular verses are part of a complex of exegetical problems regarding the structure and function of the opening chapters, the precise meaning of the key verb *pleroun,* and other related issues which need not concern us here. The point which is of prime importance to the preacher who ultimately will attempt to communicate this text involves a simple observation of grammar. This observation is of significance for the preacher as well as the exegete in so far as it suggests that the citation here of Hos. 11:1 is not specifically a "Messianic prophecy" of the coming of Jesus of Nazareth. Thus the preacher who thinks that his responsibility here is to preach about a Messianic prediction having been fulfilled will want to rethink the question of precisely where and how in this text the concept of "Messiah" comes to expression.

According to this text, Joseph, the father of Jesus, was instructed by the angel of the Lord in a dream to escape with his child and wife from Bethlehem to Egypt, because Herod was searching for the child in order to eliminate Him. Joseph obeyed, and hurried with his family to Egypt, remaining there until Herod died. The author concludes this incident by stating that this action was accomplished "in order that that which was spoken by the Lord through the prophet might be fulfilled, namely, 'Out of Egypt I called My son.' "

Certainly this is no "Messianic" prophecy in the sense of a prophet's prediction about the nature of the Messiah to come in the future age. The grammar itself makes this clear. Hosea was not looking forward to the future but backward to the past. The verb "to call" is in the aorist tense: "Out of Egypt I *called* My son." A past event is being described here. In the text of Hosea it is God who is speaking these words. The son mentioned is, of course, Israel (11:1a). The "calling out of Egypt" is a reference to the central salvation event in Israel's history, her mighty deliverance by God in the exodus from Egypt, to which Hosea refers also elsewhere.[16] The concept of the "call" of God is the language of the covenant; God called, that is, He invited and chose Israel to be His people. This covenantal calling, explicated in chs. 1 and 2 of Hosea as part of the symbolic episode of Hosea's marriage and child-naming, pointing to the rejection and ultimate acceptance of Israel by God her Father, is one of many modes (along with explicit references to the exodus event) of describing and recalling the mighty salvific act of God. In the reference to these events of the exodus and the covenant, Hosea the prophet is reinterpreting and reapplying the revelation of the past to meet the needs of the present.

Understood in this soteriological context, Hos. 11:1 can be seen to be a most important text concerning the saving activity of God. And so it was interpreted by Israel in the period of history between Hosea and Matthew. As the interpretations of the rabbinic school show, at the time when Matthew wrote, a popular notion associated with Hos. 11:1 and many other similar exodus texts was the idea that Israel's redemption from Egypt was a prefigurement of the final redemption of the Messianic age.[17]

This suggests most strongly, then, that by reference to the fulfillment of this prophetic word Matthew is indeed saying something about the Messiah. What he is saying, however, is not that some Hosean prediction about a coming Messiah has now taken place. For there never was such a prediction in the first place. Hosea referred only to the past and not the future. Rather, by applying this text (whose soteriological implications later came to be associated with the conception of the final Messianic redemption of the end time) to a decisive event in Jesus' life and by interpreting this event in the light of this text, Matthew declares the very heart of his gospel: the long-awaited Messianic age has now begun, and the saving Messiah Himself is Jesus of Nazareth. For Jesus is the son whom God the Father has led out of Egypt. As throughout the New Testament, the attributes of God's people of old are applied now to God's one Man, Jesus. All that Israel was and had been is now radically telescoped and focused on the one and only true Israelite, Jesus. Jesus is *Christos,*

---

16 Cf. Hos. 2:15, 12:13. Cf. 8:13, 12:9, 13:4 ff.

17 Cf. Hermann L. Strack and Paul Billerbeck, *Kommentar zum Neuen Testament aus Talmud und Midrasch.* 2d, unaltered ed. (Munich: C. H. Beck'sche Verlags buchhandlung, 1956), I, 85—88.

Messiah, the Bringer of God's final act of redemption! That is the message of this text.

Not only the message but also the method with which Matthew employs this Hosean text is of importance to the preacher. For here should become obvious the method in which apostolic preaching was carried out and the way in which preaching radically differs from exegesis. As Cambridge scholar C. F. D. Moule has pointed out, "the Christians began from Jesus — from his known character and mighty deeds and sayings, and his death and resurrection; and with these they went to the scriptures, and found that God's dealings with his People and his intentions for them there reflected did, in fact, leap into new significance in the light of these recent happenings. Sooner or later this was to lead, through a definition of what God had done, to something like a definition of who Jesus was." [18]

That is to say, the point of departure of the earliest Christian interpreters, the real object of their interpretation, was Jesus. Jesus, His person, teaching, and works, were their "text." In order to explain and to preach their "text" they turned to their Bible, the Old Testament, and to all the current Messianic-soteriological conceptions associated with these sacred writings. Thus in the early Christian community Jesus was described in various and sundry ways as the "Prophet of the last time," "Moses *redivivus*," the "Son of David," the "Melchizedekean Priest," the apocalyptic-eschatological "Son of Man," the enthroned "King," the "Suffering Servant," and the "Messiah."

However, their prime concern, let us repeat, their point of departure, was Jesus. This is in contradistinction to the method of modern exegesis, which begins not with present experience, in fact not even with the New Testament, but with the earliest events of revelation and then moves forward, interpreting what follows in the light of what has gone before. Thus the modern exegete, in order to understand most accurately the thought world of the New Testament, begins first with the milieu of the Old Testament. He clarifies, for instance, the idea of a Messiah in the New Testament or the implications of the exodus event in the latter Covenant by first determining the meaning they had in the former Testament. The exegete takes this historical course because this is the only way the foreign world

---

[18] *The Birth of the New Testament, Harper's New Testament Commentaries*, general ed. H. Chadwick (New York/Evanston: Harper & Row, 1962), pp. 57 f.

of the New Testament can be understood — only in the light of the Old.

However, whereas the exegete is concerned with the historical course of God's people and her relationship to Him, the preacher is not. Rather, as we learned from the New Testament, the Christian preacher, be he Matthew or any other, is interested primarily in the now, the present act of the divine drama. This is his overwhelming interest because of his conviction that Jesus is the Christ, and as such the very center, beginning, and end of all history. True, there are those such as Luke who do have an interest in history, but even for them Jesus represents the very center and pivot point of all that has been and will be. From the vantage point of modern exegesis, therefore, it would be incorrect to speak of the "exegesis" of the earliest Christian interpreters. The manner in which they treated their Biblical material was tendential and biased. The bias and tendentiousness was their conviction of faith, which colored and determined all they thought and said. Basically they were not primarily interested in interpreting the Scriptures but rather Jesus — as the Christ, the Bringer of salvation to them and their people. They were not exegetes but preachers.

Certainly this is not to suggest that this mode of interpretation is to be adopted in toto by preachers today. The Christian cannot use the current events of his own day as the text of his sermon — contrary, apparently, to the thinking of many — because for him the center of history and the point of orientation of all of life is not to be found in any event of this atomic and nominally "post-Christian" age but only in an event of the distant past. Nor do we suggest that the task of proclamation is easier than it looks or as easy as that of the preachers of the first century. In point of fact it is not. For the many gaps which separate the preacher and his audience from the events which have changed men's lives require not only bridges to be built by exegesis but also all the resources at the preacher's command for enabling the Good News which Matthew shared with his audience to become Good News for his own people as well.

Rather, we learn from this passage in Matthew's Gospel what the essential indicative of Christian preaching must be; namely, that Jesus is the Messiah, the Christ. Any contemporary preaching purporting to be a preaching of this text which results in anything less than an address to the worshiping hearers to accept and believe in this Man of Nazareth as their God-sent Redeemer from sin and the slavery of life and as the Son of God through whom they too have become the children of God — any preachment less than this is not a communication of the meaning of the Good News according to Matthew. To attempt to speak about the fulfilling of a Messianic prediction on the basis of this text is to fail to understand this text's real Messianic character.

Furthermore, we are reminded again here of the basic differences between the exegetical and homiletical tasks. As the concern of the exegete involves the place of Matthew's preaching of Jesus Christ within the history of the primitive community, so the preacher's aim is to let that preachment of Matthew preach today once again, so that today too men are called upon to praise and glorify Jesus as the Messiah of God.

Another text illumined in similar fashion by a critical study of the history of traditions is 1 Peter 2:4-10. Jesus here is designated as a stone (lithos) which has been rejected by men but is considered precious and exalted in the eyes of God (2:4). The Old Testament passages which the author cites in connection with this designation of Jesus as "stone," as well as a series of "stone" texts which span the intertestamental and New Testament writings, can be shown to belong to a particular tradition of Judaeo-Christian interpretation which attributed to these "stone" passages Messianic connotations. According to Mark 12:10-11 and parallels, furthermore, it might be suggested that Jesus Himself is responsible for the initial application of these Messianic passages to Himself. (Cf. also Acts 4:11; Rom. 9:32-33; and Eph. 2:20.) The Messianic-eschatological connotations of these "stone" passages in the New Testament and earlier Jewish literature indicate that the application of the term stone to Jesus by the author of 1 Peter constitutes fundamentally a proclamation of Jesus as the Messiah and Bringer of the eschaton. Those who believe in Him as such become as He is; they too become living "stones" (2:5); they too are precious in the sight of God (2:7). For those who reject Jesus as Messiah, who disbelieve, declares the author in a metaphorical play on words, this living and exalted Stone becomes a "stumbling stone and the rock of scandal." They stumble because they have disbelieved the Word about Him and from Him (2:7-8). Those who believe, however, become the elect race of God just as their Lord is the elect Stone of God. Thus the indicative which Peter proclaims here is essentially similar to Matthew's message: Jesus is the Messiah. In addition Peter states that the community of those who affirm this rejected "stone" as the resurrected and life-dispensing "stone" of God shall also participate in the life and favor of divine election and the mercy of the Lord whose mighty acts they proclaim.

Thus a text which is often superficially taken to speak primarily of the church as temple or of individual Christians as "kings" and "priests" before God in reality proclaims the Messiahship and exaltation of Jesus and the election and redemption of all those who declare Jesus to be Lord. A preacher has only preached the Good News of this text when he has confronted his hearers with the scandalous rock and stone of stumbling, Jesus the Christ, as their Messiah and Lord.

Finally, in order to consider the service which isagogics renders the preacher in determining where the brunt of the message is to be found, we might take the text for Quinquagesima Sunday, that perennially problematic passage, 1 Cor. 13:1-13. Each new generation brings to this text questions shaped by its own cultural and historical milieu. Whether the would-be interpreter is a hedonistic Greek of the third century or a puritanical Englishman of the 16th, as the history of Biblical interpretation has shown, makes no small difference in the interpretation of the term "love" found here. Beyond all the differences of interpretation, however, there is one important point of similarity. Contrary to the usual problem of understanding where the reader does not know the subject matter well enough, here both exegete and preacher forever face the problem of describing the meaning of 1 Cor. 13 to people who are sure that they already know all about the text. In this unusual situation isagogics performs a true service by first demonstrating that in the context of this letter love is something far different from what the average reader assumes it to be. Secondly, an isagogical consideration of this text not only alerts one to misconceptions but also clarifies the context, historical and literary, in which this so badly misunderstood word might be accurately comprehended.

An isagogical study of 1 Corinthians shows that the church to which the apostle Paul was writing was a community that had forgotten or ignored the matter of *unity* which titles such as "church" and "body" and "love" actually imply. This was a menagerie of Christians who loved to distinguish, divide, and separate. They made a practice of esteeming some and despising others, of separating Jew from Greek, simple from wise, poor from rich, weak in faith from the daringly faithful, and dividing into separate cliques, a "Paul faction," an "Apollos faction," a "Cephas faction," and even a "Christ faction." Jealousy and strife ran rampant. Moral abuses of incest and sexual laxity and litigation before the pagan courts marred the countenance of this church. Even in the worship assembly disunity and despising of the have-nots prevailed so that the Eucharistic feast of love was turned into a travesty of selfishness and the noncommunication of ecstatic language was valued more than the edifying, upbuilding message of the prophet's word. It was to such a church that St. Paul wrote this lyric on love.

The fundamental malady, the error lying at the root and center of all these manifestations of a pathetic and tragic misunderstanding of the Christian Gospel, was the false teaching of a group of Jewish-Christian fifth columnists who extolled wisdom or knowledge as the highest of all life's goals. These were men who advocated and sought a higher and more sophisticated form of knowledge (*gnosis*) than that which Paul apparently had to offer. This "gnostic" heresy was the heresy of independence, individuality, and isolationism, which claimed that "religion" was an individual affair, a solely one-to-one relationship between the individual and God. To "know" was to enter an exclusively personal and individualistic relationship with Sophia, Wisdom. Communion with the fellowman was not only unnecessary, it was a hindrance to the attainment of perfection. The goal of the "gnostic" was an exclusive communion of his soul with its cosmic source and the soaring transcendence of the realm of the material world of flesh-and-blood living.

As literary analysis further shows, Paul's answer to this malignant display of lovelessness, bigotry, and division-mongering is to preach once again about the divine *sophia,* the "foolishness of the cross," the Good News of the gift of union and communion with God and man in and through Jesus Christ. He unfolds the essence and meaning of what it means to be the church, the new resurrected body of Christ. Against all condescenders and enthusiasts for the due processes of law, against the rich who despise the poor and those who prize the mystery of tongues above the edification of the prophetic Word, against all who seek a profounder "wisdom" and trample on their fellowmen in their quest, Paul assures that there is only *one Gospel,* Jesus Christ the Crucified; only *one Giver* of all gifts, the Holy Spirit;

and only *one Source* of all things in this creation, the almighty and sovereign God alone. The life that a man has to enjoy is no more and no less than a union and communion with this God and His total reunited and recommuned creation.

These are the themes which lead up to and surround St. Paul's lofty lyric on love. Only in this context will chapter 13 yield its basic meaning. For here all these themes reach their zenith. Man's total task as member of the redeemed and resurrected community is presented in the possibility of nurturing this union and communion. The highest expression of this task and the goal toward which man in this in-between period of the "already and not yet" paradoxically can only strive, and can never perfectly reach, the task which ultimately only God Himself can accomplish, is the "way which supersedes all else" — the way of love. This chapter not only summarizes what has gone before but also anticipates both the theme of edification in ch. 14 and the message of resurrection victory and the nature of the new man in ch. 15. The things mentioned here in ch. 13, the gift of tongues and prophecy, the possession of knowledge *(gnosis),* self-sacrifice, the positive traits of love and love's negative counterparts, and finally the unique permanence and perfection of love — all concepts and phenomena in connection with which love is discussed and described — are direct reflections of the concerns and problems of the Corinthian community. As Karl Barth has accurately indicated: "Once we lose sight of the sentimental-moral misunderstanding of the word 'love,' there is, apart from [ch.] xv., no chapter in the whole epistle wherein Paul has expressed in such radical terms, and with such incisive severity, what he had to urge in a critical spirit against the Corinthian Christians." [19]

In the final analysis, the observation of careful isagogical analysis will save the preacher from making of love something sentimental rather than eschatological. It will show Paul's answer to be that love is a divine gift, not a human virtue. This is to say that it will ultimately enable the preacher to preach what should be preached — the love made manifest at Golgotha which makes all human loving possible, the scandal of the cross where one finally learns "what fools we mortals be."

In summary, all the observations concerning the relationship

[19] Karl Barth, *The Resurrection of the Dead* (New York: Fleming H. Revell, 1933), pp. 83 f.

between preaching and hermeneutics, exegesis, and isagogics, and all
the Biblical texts examined to illustrate this relationship seem to
point to one fundamental issue or concern. This is the question
whether the preacher of today is communicating to his contemporaries
precisely and exclusively what the inspired author intended to communicate in the first place. Is that which the contemporary preacher
says the message *means* today in very fact identical to that which the
text *meant* as it first came into being at the author's hand? Or to
reverse the question, Is that meaning and message which exegetical
analysis finds in a particular text in very fact the same message and
meaning which eventually gets communicated in every sermon on
that text? If Christian preaching today is to remain faithful to the
intention of all of Holy Scripture, then each sermon will necessarily
involve a direct and unavoidable confrontation of the hearers with the
divine Word of judgment and pardon, destruction and deliverance,
to which each individual hearer must necessarily respond, "This is
God's Word *pro me,* for me!" Still more specifically, for Christian
preachers and their audiences the real crux of the matter must ever
and always be nothing less than the crux of Calvary. Such preaching
must amount to a challenge to the hearer, who must take a position
over against this saving event.

As has become evident in the three Biblical texts examined, the
basic issue at stake in all the New Testament and the question which
every inspired author-preacher posed, directly or indirectly, to his
hearers was this: Do you believe that Jesus is the Christ, the Messiah,
the eschatological Bringer of the Kingdom and the Redeemer-Recon-
ciler of all men including yourself? Are you worshiping God as God
by acclaiming and affirming Jesus as His Son and your Lord?

In an article whose subject is much related to ours, "The Significance of Isagogics for Sermon Preparation," Münster New Testament
scholar Willi Marxen summarized this significance as both a burden
and a blessing.[20] The burden which Marxen sees isagogics bringing
to all sermon preparation is the constant reminder of what we have
called the gap which separates the preacher from the text, the gap
which necessitates sound exegesis as the bridge for proper understanding. More precisely, this burden involves an awareness of the fact
that the Biblical pericope which the preacher takes as his text itself

---

[20] Willi Marxen, "Die Bedeutung der Einleitungswissenschaft für die
Predigtarbeit," *Monatschrift für Pastoraltheologie,* XLIX (1960), 1—14, esp. 13.

intended to be no "text" at all but rather a sermon on another text. Thus the task of exegetical sermon preparation involves a complicated series of checks and inquiries into the various stages this portion of the Christian tradition experienced, the really basic original text (Jesus is the Christ), and the various modes of interpretation and application to new situations which this basic text received until it reached the shape and form in which the preacher now sees and knows it.

In reality, this "burden" of tradition criticism is the responsibility of first appreciating how the basic Christian proclamation was reformulated and reworded to meet new situations, or how the Christians of the first century understood and treated their texts, before one is in a position to make that text understandable and applicable anew. The burden of the preacher, then, constitutes not merely an acknowledgement of the need for exegetical study in sermon preparation but also the very exercise of that exegesis. As our exegetical probings have attempted to demonstrate, only in this way will the preacher be able to stand confidently before his people and be assured that to the best of his ability he is communicating nothing less than *God's* Word — the counsel of God, the whole counsel of God, and nothing but the counsel of God.

But exegesis is not merely the burden of knowing the history of the text. Exegesis — in Marxen's discussion isagogics in particular — affords a substantial relief. The text ceases to dominate and demand — not only in the sense that certain things have to "get said" in a certain and unchanging way but also in the very vocabulary and imagery used. For hermeneutics, exegesis, and isagogics teach the preacher that he should feel free to express the Biblical message in the manner — no matter how possibly strange to the ears of a first-century Christian — in which that message best "gets across," best "gets through." When the preacher who has so come to know what his text once meant is able to communicate that text with such a freedom under the Spirit so that it "hits home" as living Word once again, then and only then will he be preaching not general and irrelevant truths but rather *the* truth of God's will and Word *for his congregation.*

It is this task and this goal of letting God's Word be God's Word for God's people today to which our beloved teacher and father in Christ has devoted his entire ministry and life. The scheme and procedure of sermon preparation which he has been teaching at Concordia Seminary, and through which he has been changing for the good the preaching patterns of our entire church, incorporates all the exegetical *Vorarbeit* of which we have been speaking. By Caemmerer the prospective preacher is directed not primarily to topics but to texts, Biblical texts. There he is urged to view that section of Scripture through the Lutheran hermeneutical looking glass of Law and Gospel. He is encouraged to find in that text a goal for the hearer, a diagnosis of human (including the hearer's) malady, and also a statement concerning the divine power serving as the means to the goal.

Admittedly there are points where the critical exegete might not find himself in full agreement with the Caemmererian system. Certainly the question whether the process — as outlined, for instance, in his basic work, *Preaching for the Church* — emphasizes adequately enough the significance of the original historical situation of the Biblical text would be a valid one. For though Caemmerer stresses that the preacher must first ask, "What was the original speaker or writer trying to accomplish for his listeners or readers?" in the following lines he appears to allow for an "indirect method" in which the preacher would "utilize an idea in a text toward a goal for which the text was not originally written" (p. 69). Though he acknowledges that such a step is often a last resort and a substitute for patient exegesis or the ability to locate a text to suit his purpose, it must seriously be asked if such a method is to be tolerated at all. For in such a way is the Bible not reduced from the living Word into a handy but lifeless stock of texts?

Or the exegete concerned with the particular formulation of the Gospel within a particular document might object to the "importation" of either goal, malady, or means from other contexts. Does not such a promiscuous use of parallel passages — the hermeneutical principle of interpreting within the total context of Scripture notwithstanding — hinder if not prohibit a more careful scrutiny of the particular context for clues? Keeping in mind that the Word of God is always a word directed to a particular situation, exactly how hermeneutically sound is the practice of "filling in" or interpreting a text from 2 Peter with material taken from the historically earlier and quite different context of 1 Thessalonians or even Mark 9?

Finally, one might ask if the categories of "goal, malady, and means" are always the most adequate ones for analyzing the text.

Do all Biblical pericopes fit such a categorization and, if not, are they for this reason inadequate as sermon texts? This is not to deny that in general these three factors afford an excellent vantage point for preaching the message of the text. Nor is this to question the validity of the Law/Gospel distinction which is at the basis of this categorization, at least as concerns the preacher (many exegetes no doubt would object strenuously that to approach the text with this set of questions alone is to straitjacket it and often to submit to the text questions which it is not prepared or intended to answer). Rather this is only to ask whether such texts as Ps. 23 or 100 or Col. 1:15-20, for example, are best studied in preparation and presented in sermon according to the categories of goal, malady, and means.

But these are specific questions which are addressable to Caemmerer's system only because this system is based on certain assumptions about which there is absolutely no disagreement; namely, the necessary nexus between exegesis and homiletics. And this in turn points to the profoundest of all concerns: that the Good News of God's reconciling activity in Jesus Christ become the Good News for people again and again. Good news is news which is good for particular people in particularly bad situations. That which makes true and accurate Christian proclamation *good* news is the manner in which it corrects, ameliorates, and restores the old and the bad back to the new and the good. It is this fundamental emphasis of Caemmerer's on what he calls the "for-you-ness" of the Christian message [21] which puts him in the company of the prophets of Israel and the preachers of the primitive church, and of the exegetes today who would fully appreciate the proclamation of both. As far as the central concern of Christian proclamation is concerned, what Caemmerer has said in one way — preaching is God's Word in Christ to and for people — Bultmann has said in another: "It is the Word of God because it confronts me with his mercy and grace. . . . This is why it is a word addressed *realiter* to me on a specific occasion, whether it be in the Church's proclamation, or in the Bible mediated through the Church as the Word of God addressed to me, or through the word of my fellow Christian. That is why the living Word of God is never a word of human wisdom but an event encountered in history. . . . This event is Jesus Christ." [22]

21 *Preaching for the Church,* p. 51.
22 *Kerygma and Myth,* p. 207.

This is precisely the mode of the New Testament preachment: good news for and addressed to people. As Heidelberg scholar Günther Bornkamm has pointed out concerning the preaching of Paul: "It is characteristic of Pauline preaching . . . that despite clear points of contact with concepts and forms of thought and style of particularly the Diaspora synagogue, this preaching is in no way bound to the rigid scheme of other missionary preaching with its stereotyped arrangement of themes; nor does it proceed in apologetic-paedagogical fashion (as, e. g., Acts 17!). Rather, at every moment it confronts the hearer himself with the message of salvation and attempts to convince him in this his situation before the punishing and pardoning Word of God." [23] Matt. 2; 1 Cor. 13; and 1 Peter 2 have shown that this method of homiletical application of the message to the human situation so that it becomes good news is typical for the rest of the New Testament as well. From the vantage point of exegesis, no higher tribute could be paid a preacher than this: In the purest sense of the New Testament Gospel, his preaching was indeed Good News all over again!

Thirty-four years ago the internationally renowned Biblical scholar and historian Hans Lietzmann, in a preface explaining the addition of a volume of homiletical analyses to the historically, literary, and linguistically oriented commentary *Handbuch zum Neuen Testament,* made this observation:

> Ich sehe wohl die Not unserer Kirche, wenn exegetische Wissenschaft, theologische Systematik und kirchliche Praxis auseinanderfallen, wenn der junge Theologe auf der Kanzel mit alledem nichts anzufangen weiss, was er auf der hohen Schule gelernt hat. Unsere Kirche braucht biblische Predigt mehr als je. Und wenn unserer heutige exegetische Wissenschaft nicht imstande wäre, die lebendigen Kräfte des Evangeliums besser ergreifen zu lehren als die Wissenschaft früherer Zeiten, so wäre sie ein tönend Erz oder eine klingende Schelle. Aber freilich, an der praktischen Verwertung dieser Erkenntnis fehlt noch viel. Und darum habe ich einen Kollegen um Hilfe gebeten, der durch lange Jahre in der kirchlichen Praxis bewährt ist und den Beweis geliefert hat, dass eine auf strengster exegetischer und historischer Grundlage aufgebaute und dann das Wesen der Sache scharf erfassende Predigt auf die Menschen der Gegenwart gewaltig zu wirken vermag. [24]

One might wish to speculate how the tragic subsequent history

---

[23] *Die Religion in Geschichte und Gegenwart,* 3. Auflage, hrsg. von K. Galling (Tübingen, J. C. B. Mohr, 1958), II, 1004.

[24] Vorwort zum *Handbuch zum Neuen Testament,* Band 22: Die Alten Perikopen, von Leonhard Fendt (Tübingen, J. C. B. Mohr, 1931), pp. vi—vii.

of Germany might have been affected or even altered if more exegetes
and preachers had been sympathetic to Lietzmann's concern. But
such speculation, however interesting, would be idle. The task of
the church today is not to speculate about the past but to see that
what was destructive in the past is eliminated or altered for good
in the present and future. There are voices who raise the same fears
about breaches and gaps today which Lietzmann raised over three
decades ago. Certainly there can be no question about how the church
and all of God's people are best served. The gaps must be bridged.
For the Good News to be recognized and proclaimed as news which
is good, the Gospel, exegesis and preaching must operate hand in
hand. To this the teacher and preacher whose gift to the church
we here acknowledge would only say, "Amen." May many more rise
up to join him.

PART IV

"The new concerns with a theology of the First Article spur to a mode of restating a theology of Three Articles indivisible."

The Church in the World

MARTIN E. MARTY

If the whole of a *Festschrift* honors a man, so may its parts. My part, therefore, begins with a personal word of gratitude to Richard R. Caemmerer for his efforts for the church. Just as his portion of the church experienced an evangelical awakening partly because of the fruits of his teaching, so did the generation of his students to which I belong. On the Concordia campus I may never have been classified as a "Caemmererian." The evening discussions in his crowded study seemed too advanced and arcane for my immature ears. But his classroom influence was outstanding. During the 23 years that I was enrolled in school somewhere or other I count myself fortunate to have had four or five great teachers — a higher average than most students count, I am told — and in that company Professor Caemmerer's place would never be challenged.

For his setting forth of the evangelical teaching to us, he was to our generation not only *il miglior fabbro,* the better craftsman, but also the spiritual father. The seminary was understaffed, its professors overworked in the early years after World War II. So each of us saw a great deal of our chosen mentors. The years 1948—52 were exciting years at Concordia. The beginnings of ecumenical experience were evident. The besieged faculty responded courageously to criticism. At the center of criticism and response was the man who never welcomed the role, Professor Caemmerer. The role brought out his most creative abilities, and we were the rewarded ones.

But if personal gratitude were to be the topic of each chapter in this book, the authors would do better to send a greeting card to the honoree or to raise funds for a bronze plaque for his office door. Instead we have been invited to write critical articles picking up themes associated with Caemmerer's name and to do what he would much prefer. We are to engage in conversation with his treatment of these themes, hopefully with some prospect of benefit to the church.

Richard Caemmerer's treatment of the theme "The Church in the World" has been so clear, so succinct, so pointed, that it has deserved a wider hearing outside his own church body. One of the tragedies of his career has been that he began to teach one generation before his denomination was sufficiently in the public arena and in the ecumenical circle to permit its sons to be heard. One of the delights of the ensuing generation has been to profit from his efforts to bring us into that arena and that circle and to "trade on his capital" of theological wisdom. From this point, therefore, I shall no longer discuss a personal involvement with Professor Caemmerer. Instead, pursuing my vocation as a church historian (who is supposed to try to set events into context) and as a book reviewer (who is supposed to take a specific document seriously), I wish to discuss the substantial contribution of Caemmerer to the church-world debate and to comment on where the subject is leading us today. For this his book *The Church in the World* serves admirably. From the first edition of 1949 through the third, revised printing in 1961 he has let its argument stand as a condensation of countless courses, seminars, and developments of his position in other writings and lectures. It deserves careful attention.

I

The church? "The Church stands in darkness, in this time of her pilgrimage, and must lament under many miseries" (St. Augustine). Caemmerer's position of love and loyalty to the church finds him standing with the church in its darkness, its pilgrimage, its miseries. If her sons can "help" her, Caemmerer for one would do so through his view of the church.

The world? "The world affirms itself automatically" (Albert Schweitzer). Caemmerer's position of criticism and rejection of the world finds him standing against the self-affirming world. The sentence of Schweitzer could mean two things. It could mean that the

world as created order and under God's creative care is so full of
potentiality that its self-affirmation is obvious and needs no help.
It could also mean that the world as people is consumed with the
enterprise of self-justification and needs no help from the church
for this task. Caemmerer, for one, would give it no help through his
view of the world.

The church in the world? "The city of God is made by the
love of God pushed to the contempt of self; the earthly city by love
of self, pushed to the contempt of God." Once again I resort to
Augustine to describe Caemmerer's attitude. The earthly city or the
world, he says, always stands only in opposition to the church. The
church lives in the domain of life, while the world is "dead . . . with
the death of the absence of God" (p. 101). Never in the book do
we find a world-affirming theological assertion, though we do find,
as I propose to note later, some clues or comments which suggest that
the author depicts certain contexts in which the world ought to be
affirmed.

Were the radical church/world separation the only point to
Caemmerer's work, one could easily dismiss it or summarize it as
propaganda for asceticism and withdrawal. But since he reveals no
trace of interest in withdrawal, a subtler issue is at stake, and we are
inspired to isolate it. Here it is important to begin to set this specific
work into context. I have heard Caemmerer students say that they
think of him first of all as the one "who opened up the whole world
for them." Whoever reads this book without having known Caemmerer or having read his other works would be at a loss to find any
theological lines or exegetical comments which open up any feature
of the world.

Caemmerer's substantial position can be summarized in three
of his book titles. On the one hand is *Preaching for the Church.* (At
this apparent pole one can see his less significant works: *Christ Builds
His Church, Feeding and Leading,* and *God's Great Plan for You.*)
At the other "pole" one would be tempted to set *The Church in the
World.* Holding the two together or setting up creative tension between the two would be his Christological work (now out of print),
The Atoning Christ, a series of Lenten sermons which will probably
turn out to be the nearest to a systematic theological statement we
shall receive from his hand.

I have used "apparent pole" or have set the word *pole* in quotation marks to indicate that we do not have a polarity but an extension. *The Church in the World's* argument stands in tension at no point with the books on upbuilding the church. It is not the book one would expect on the doctrine of God or Creation, or a book of Christian ethics, and certainly not of a world-affirmation which would somehow complicate the development of thought about upbuilding, nurturing, equipping, and edifying the church. *The Church in the World* is only a development of the theme of a one-theme man. It illustrates how rich has been his comment on that theme and how single-minded he has been in concentrating on it. There is everything for the church and nothing for the world in this book. It is a manual of arms, an enchiridion, a handbook of strategy for the Christian soldier in his battle with the world; it is no Baedeker or catalog of earthly delights, and it provides no theological programme for understanding them.

To set the book thus in context is in no way a criticism of Caemmerer. He has done what any author has a right to do: He set forth clearly what he was going to talk about and then he talked about it single-mindedly. "Can [the Christian churches] discover new techniques and strategies for strengthening their own hand and improving their attack? This book proposes to redefine and apply the strategy which the New Testament suggests. The author makes no apology for advocating this ancient concept" (from the Preface, unpaged). But to see this context is to see the need for a reminder: that those for whom Caemmerer "opened up the world" are deriving their impression from his personal attitudes, from portions of his theology which he has developed but casually or incidentally, or at least (since I have not heard or read his every word) not from anything theologically integral to this his considered statement on the world. Those who rely only on this book, therefore, will not understand what his students have meant. Those who rely on this book will, if they are patient, experience a wonderful awakening as Christians doing battle with the world which Caemmerer (following the Gospel) does not open, but which he closes.

The context is first of all exegetical. Caemmerer is an accomplished church historian and an alert observer of contemporary life. But *The Church in the World* finds him treating church history through casual and sometimes dangerous generalizations. He seems generally bored by contemporary cultural analysis. The 16 titles or authors chosen for reference or for recommended further reading seem to have been selected almost arbitrarily. Caemmerer seems to be telling us that in his context at the moment none of this should be taken too seriously. The strength of this book is its interpretation of the Bible; in a 100-page book there are over 450 citations from Scripture — almost five per page. None of them are used as static "prooftexts" or dead categories: each substantiates his argument and is integral to it just as his interpretation flows from and is not imposed on the text. If non-Biblical evidence is to count at all, it will have to be highly secondary in any argument on ground rules established by Caemmerer, who is at home in Scripture by intuition and by design.

Not that the author makes no contemporary comment or that he has no interest in the empirical world, the domain of our effective lives. When he talks about the world's 'flesh' — a favorite category for him — he seems to invite us to empirical inquiry, as did the "Christian Questions and Their Answers" which we used to have to memorize in Catechism class. What if we do not experience need? What about such a man?

> To such a person no better advice can be given than that, in the first place, he put his hand into his bosom, and feel whether he still have flesh and blood. . . .
>
> Secondly, that he look around to see whether he is still in the world. . . .
>
> Thirdly, he will certainly have the devil also about him, who with his lying and murdering, day and night, will let him have no peace within or without. . . . (A Short Explanation of Dr. Martin Luther's Small Catechism, St. Louis: Concordia Publishing House [1943], p. 35)

But Caemmerer does not really base argument on the empirical tests of touch, vision, and measurement. He moves on readily to the second half of the three observations: ". . . and that he by all means believe what the Scriptures say of it . . . as the Scriptures say . . . as the Scriptures picture him. . . ." One could wish that Caemmerer would regard many kinds of evidence more satisfying to humans in their complexity than he does. The fact remains that he does not; one must turn elsewhere for such evidence. He will convince, convict, and compel only through the Word as it is heard in Scripture.

Second, the exegetical context is that of the New Testament. Again, Caemmerer has told us that is his context, and he should not be criticized for his choice. It is up to those who wish to do systematic and constructive work on the whole church-world relationship to remember that he deals little with the Old Testament (about 25 sweeping references), which is also the Word of God for the church, and which also says more things and other things about the world than does the New. Over 60 percent of the Scriptural references are from the New Testament letters, and almost 70 turn us to Paul's Corinthian letters. It would hardly be unfair to say that when Caemmerer discusses "The Church in the World" he writes a commentary on First and Second Corinthians and he speaks meaningfully to the church wherever it shares and insofar as it shares any feature of the life of the Christian community in the Corinthian kind of setting. If he chose to discuss other settings his story would be more complicated. Fortunately for him (though not necessarily for the church or the world) the Corinthian picture can be applied with deadly accuracy to the church in many ages of the past and many situations of the present. He is not dealing with an obscure side issue but with a central theme.

Third, he reads the situation of the church in the world through Lutheran spectacles. Luther and the 16th-century Confessions are not referred to in Caemmerer's sources. Perhaps this was a disciplined and studied avoidance for a Luther scholar and a Luther confessor. He has worked during the years of the Luther renaissance and in the presence of many students and colleagues who might be described as "neoconfessionalists." It often has seemed to me that he did not always let us see his spectacles so that he could help us see what he saw through them; he seemed to resist subtly the devotion to Luther and the Confessions when their advocates seemed to let them stand in the line of vision to the Word in Scripture. (Needless to say, I cannot prove this observation to everyone's satisfaction, or I would set out to do so!) It is again important to remember the context: Caemmerer is not trying to say everything which the church catholic has said or even ought to say on the church-world topic. He is consciously and unconsciously a Lutheran confessor looking through Pauline eyes at the reality of the church. Therefore he does not make extended comment on any independent doctrine of God or doctrine of creation as a means of understanding the world. Indeed, as a Lutheran it is not likely that he could conceive of an "independent" doctrine or want to develop a doctrine of creation. He sees the creation *sub specie Christi.*

By now the fourth feature of Caemmerer's context is clear: His discussion of "The Church in the World" is always and only not merely Christological but *soteriological.* He has no substantial and integral interest other than "salvation." We should not be surprised at this nor should he be faulted for carrying out his intention, but once again we must be reminded that this is his intention. He sees everything *in loco justificationis,* in the light of the doctrine of justification or better — for he resists static categories — in the aspect of man being brought to wholeness and health and salvation by the activity of God in the atoning Christ. This means that he sees everything, literally everything, in the scope of a cosmic drama. He acknowledges that there are other ways of seeing things and speaking about them, but to admit them into his work would obscure his urgent point for the church: "Don't you know there's a war on?"

"We are not in first place concerned with the menace of the world or the challenge of the world, but the people of the world" (p. 2). These people are subjects and objects of the cosmic drama of salvation. "We study the world, therefore, to discover what it is about the world that makes it so much . . . in need of rescue by the church" (p. 14). "We saw that the world is not merely the space of created things; not merely the sum total of people in the world; but people moved only by earthly things, subject to the forces of man and devil hostile to God, and themselves hostile." (P. 14)

For Caemmerer such a view of salvation does not mean that "the church, in its attack, seeks . . . to herd the people of the world into concentration camps labeled 'church'" (p. 77), though many might read things that way and many in his own church body have often spoken of world and church in such terms. No, the church is in the world for a reason: for witness and love and service. But in each case these are seen soteriologically and only so. Who can argue with this? Does the church really have more than one thing to do and to say? The church of Christ knows that man is not free if he must "affirm himself," if he must engage in self-justification or — in Paul's concrete picture — in "boasting." His wholeness and health are interpreted and climaxed in salvation in Christ, a salvation which has eternal *and* temporal implications. The Lutheran answers: No, the church does not have other things to say or do than to save. The question is complicated only when one wants to render "salvation" concrete and to rescue it from abstraction, formula, and mere verbalization. The corollaries and the details of the salvation drama are infinitely complex. Caemmerer wants us to keep our eye on the main plot, and he refers to as few of these details and corollaries as possible, or as necessary.

As a Doctor of the Gospel Caemmerer has succeeded in warding off both the legalism or the antinomianism which can afflict the church and the Lutheran churches when they leave the evangelical center. No one can read and be convinced by *The Church in the World* without sharing in the exhilaration of the evangelical experience, but no one can use this exhilaration as an inspirer of libertinism!

II

In Caemmerer's exegetical context the church is pictured ideally. By this I do not mean that the church is for him an abstraction. With the Lutheran Confessions he regularly affirms what they say: "We are not dreaming about some Platonic republic . . . but we teach that this church actually exists, made up of true believers and righteous men scattered throughout the world."* Rather Caemmerer always begins by asserting the ideal intention for the church which exists in history but whose real life is hid with Christ in God. He reasons from that assertion; he never begins phenomenologically with an analysis of the empirical situation. Like all good Lutherans, his sociology of the church is dominated by the theological norm and not vice versa. The church is people, the author never tires of asserting. These people are sinners. But the real life of these sinners is the healthy, whole, saved, and fulfilled life of the forgiven.

These proper exegetical assertions often lead the reader to conclude that Caemmerer will be tempted to minimize the faults of the church. Not so. His book could for much of the course be described by the title "The World in the Church." A reader could underline every critical reference to the church in these 100 pages, could reorganize them in systematic fashion, and he could have a highly condensed outline which anticipates every major finding of the sociological criticism of the churches of the kind that came into vogue in the 1950s. Caemmerer could not conceivably be surprised by any finding of the sociologists concerning the weakness, the faithlessness,

* Ap VIII 20. *The Book of Concord: The Confessions of the Evangelical Lutheran Church,* trans. and ed. Theodore G. Tappert in collaboration with Jaroslav Pelikan, Robert H. Fischer, and Arthur C. Piepkorn (Philadelphia: Muhlenberg [Fortress] Press, 1959), p. 171.

the sinfulness of church members. He could read them all and find no feature of his view of the church changed.

Are all readers capable of sustaining both sides of his vision? The countless references to the faults of the church do not stick in the mind; they come as abstractions and they hardly "do their job." The resultant temptation is that one may carry away an implausibly hopeful view of the church based on Caemmerer's view of its actual focality in the world. His view of the parish or the family may be theologically asserted but cannot in the 1960s be sociologically verified. Thus he can in one sentence remind us properly: "The needy world reacts with double hostility to a church which fosters the same blindness to need which the world itself has; and there are many such churches" (p. 61). Do we not also need to be reminded that every survey turned up in the real, the actual world shows that the churches have been the *centers* of resistance to racial change; that they have often *designedly* organized life in such a way that they screen off the vision of human need; that in all such surveys the most active and orthodox church members are the least open to the understanding of the whole world's needs; that the agnostic, the humanitarian, or the Jewish communities ordinarily shame the "loving activities" of the Christian communities busy with talk about salvation and the all-engrossing institutional inversion which preoccupies them? Caemmerer knows all this and in tantalizingly brief and generalizing statements tells us this. He follows the stated definition and intention of his book. But his students who carried his generalizations into detailed empirical observation have led us to view church and world somewhat differently in their practical vocational lives than they would if they worked only with his exegetical picture. In this sense corollary pictures of the church-world relationship developed by Caemmerer's students look and seem somewhat different from the strictly theological view presented in this book.

If Caemmerer's picture of the church therefore seems to be practically unrealistic to people caught at the crossroads of church and world, what about his picture of the world? Since his focus is soteriological, as we have noted, it can always and only be totally negative. The slightest affirmation about the world, about people, about the created order's potentiality, when asserted *in loco justificationis* would break apart the whole evangelical teaching. It would make Christ's death unnecessary and thus absurd and would be the ultimate denial. In Caemmerer's view therefore the "world" is an abstraction for people who are materialist, motivated by lust, marked by unbelief. Those words are repeated to characterize the world with almost wearying frequency, and properly so. Whether or not Caemmerer should have excluded from his topic all reference to "world" as Biblical representative of the created order or as sphere where Christ's lordship is present outside the strictly soteriological question is not the point here: We need simply remember that Caemmerer has chosen to rule out such reference. We are left to shift for ourselves then, theologically, to make sense of God's activity in the world apart from the question of salvation in the direct and almost narrow sense of the term.

For this reason, just as Caemmerer's generalizations about the church's problematics led his students into empirical analysis, so his focal view of the world as soteriological problem has led them to try to extend his "doctrine of the world" and to see its relation to other aspects of Christian teaching. Needless to say such inquiry does not turn up a Polyanna-like picture of "the good world." Whatever else the 20th century — the century of Buchenwald and the hard sell, of racial oppression and exploitative propaganda, of two world wars and ten trillion evidences of hate — needs, it does not need a deluding picture of the actuality of the world. But Christians in the world *do* need a theological rationale for every aspect of their vocation in it just as Caemmerer provides one for their saving witness against it.

To take a picture from the psychological experience of a Caemmerer student. He carries away a picture which reveals the Christian parish to be a center of witness, of loving and saving service. Such a student has ministered in the last decade of racial change. He preaches the saving Gospel, uses the right words, is a model of diplomacy and tact. But he finds that his good members are in no way open to seeing the implications of the Christian view of man and love in their dealings with other races. They are and they want to remain the center of community prejudice and hatred. The familiarity of this experience is so common it needs no documentation. The minister does not set out to excommunicate such Christians who want to thwart God's purposes for His every creature. Meanwhile the minister finds himself working with civil rights groups, the B'nai B'rith, the local human relations council, the church federation, and

a varied set of agnostic humanitarians. *They* seem to him to be effect-
ing God's purposes for His world in a way congruent with the Christian view of man and love. What is he to make of all this?

Caemmerer would not dismiss such a problem with a sneer to
the effect that we should not let psychology and observation get in the
way of theological good sense. He would relate it to the central
theological doctrine and — this book provides clues — enlarge the
concept of what "salvation" is to help cover or interpret the problem.
To my knowledge, however, he has not worked to provide an extensive theological rationale to cover the dimension or breadth of such
problems. Again and again he reminds Christians of the urgency
of their work in such domains without setting forth an interpretation
of their existence as they do so. I shall quote some instances:

> The world of business and occupation is a further field for love.
> Here again the field is so fertile because love is so unusual there. . . .
>
> Citizenship and life in the community under law is another area
> in which Chrisian love achieves witness. Again, history conspires to
> make this witness unusually fruitful, because the opportunities are so
> abundant. Despite the counsel of Romans 13 and 1 Peter 2, the Chris-
> tian church has frequently withdrawn the impulse of love from the life
> of citizenship; it has taught the believer to escape to an inner or future
> world instead of equipping him to meet the demands of community life
> with the grace of God. (Pp. 45—46)
>
> [The Christian] has to be closely enough related to the worldling,
> as a neighbor or co-worker in occupation, that he can give a demonstra-
> tion of awareness of higher values; that he can demonstrate serenity
> under the thrust of insecurity and change which continues to menace the
> materialist; and that he can show concern for the other's welfare unique
> in a world of selfish intent upon personal gain. . . . (P. 62)
>
> Thus the corporate character of the church, in small or larger group-
> ings, will be one of delight in the ways of God, in the enjoyment of His
> gifts of beauty, in the contentment with His bonuses of good cheer. . . .
> (P. 84)
>
> [The intellectual groups] seemingly have no needs of life to an-
> swer. . . . Only in recent years with the upswing in college education,
> have we found ourselves considering them as a class at all. They seem
> even more baffling and impervious to the conditioning of Christian love
> than the animalistic masses; for they are sensitive to art and aesthetics;
> many of them have their codes of morality and kindliness; many of them
> manage to live serenely and pleasantly. (P. 63)

Students have known Caemmerer to be uncommonly active at the
side of Christian and non-Christian alike in causes of community
betterment and in areas of aesthetic sensitivity. They would, I con-

tend, profit from a systematic and articulated view of how he relates this to his vision of church and world. Injunctions to "do likewise" mean less than rationales on exegetical and traditional grounds for doing so.

If none of this can be done; if the doctrines of God, of creation, of sanctification, of lordship have nothing to say as corollaries of the *locus justificationis,* then we dare not pretend that they do or can. If they cannot be derived from Biblical sources this must be frankly admitted. If one must go outside the Lutheran tradition in the ecumenical church to learn of other Biblical emphases, this must be recognized. I am not sure, however, that we have exhausted inquiry on these lines; or rather, I am sure that we have not. We have often done our theological work inside a corral. Two sides of it have been erected by those who work in the interest of an almost legalistic confessionalism which would not permit inquiry into corollaries of the soteriological doctrine. The other two sides are representative of the opacity with which "the world" of agnostics, humanitarians, Jews, legislators, artists, academicians, etc., has been viewed. Caemmerer was himself captive neither of the narrowed doctrinal view nor of cultural blindness. Nor are his students or more and more of the church body in which most of them work. Perhaps we have not exhausted the quest because we have hardly begun it. Were I a systematic theologian I could hardly picture a more engrossing, urgent, or promising task. As a historian and observer I may note that if the project is not in capable hands it will be undertaken by less capable ones; might one hope that a Richard R. Caemmerer could devote himself to setting forth a more comprehensive view of "the world" in the light of the questions the church asks today?

III

What has happened to make the question of church and world urgent or different today from what it was a quarter of a century ago when Caemmerer began his systematic work? During these years all Christians have become increasingly conscious of the scope of secularization. More and more areas of life are seen to "round themselves off" without reference to God as an explanatory feature. The world is seen as an entity to itself. More and more dimensions of life are seen in matter-of-fact, "worldly" terms; the revival of religion in recent years often served only to gloss over the process while

actually it tended to speed it up and license it. This is not to say that
the church necessarily has to count for less in the world now; I imag-
ine that for a variety of reasons Christianity is more often front-page
news now than a quarter of a century ago. But the relations of church
to world have grown increasingly complex, problematic, and promising.

For one thing the pace of ecumenical talk has increased and
Christians have seen more and more of a common destiny in the
world. The fact that Christians are a dwindling minority, a diaspora
in the world, changes the vision of the world which prevailed when
separate religious cultures were granted real isolation. *The Church
in the World* was and remains an ecumenical book. Professor Caemmerer, while he reflected the cultural history of "our own church body"
(a phrase he uses repeatedly) cannot picture speaking of part of the
Christian enterprise or destiny independently of the whole. This feature of his work produced some frustration, for his ecumenical picture
(pp. 8, 78, 100) was in no way permitted to be exercised by his students in the earlier years of his work. They had described to them
a picture of ecumenical action and were denied actual ecumenical
participation, a problem Caemmerer recognized personally but with
which he does not deal specifically in this book. In any case, he
spoke most clearly to the church in the mood of its first half century
of renewed ecumenical inquiry, when the question was how to "Let
the Church Be the Church."

Today ecumenical conversation has moved to the point where
it concerns the problem of world religions and, more notably, the
understanding of the secular world. "Let the Church Be for the
World" would be the more frequent call today. It is in this context
that the new inquiry is being undertaken. There is no danger that
the earlier form will be displaced or superseded or that it will be
forgotten or will not need to be recalled. The new creation is to
be evident each day; the attack on the old creation is therefore daily
necessary, and the freshness of the Gospel's address to the miracle
of the new creation is welcomed daily. But in addition to this evangelical message there will be more and more devotion to theological
understanding of the world's potential under the lordship of Christ.
I will point to some of the directions such inquiry may take or is
taking and to some of the resources open to it.

A. The whole Bible. The Bible, to the Lutheran Christian like

Caemmerer, is the cradle in which Christ lies; the whole Scripture is seen in the light of His saving activity. Creation and eschatology are read from this center. But a comprehensive doctrine of church-world relationships will concern itself with features of Biblical thought dismissed by Caemmerer in his hurry to come to soteriology. The Old Testaments, John 1, Rom. 8, Col. 1 — these and many other Scriptural texts relate the doctrine of creation to the Christological witness. Biblical themes having to do with stewardship of the earth, dominion over it, celebration of lordship in it, eucharist for it, identification with it, must be related to the doctrine of salvation.

B. While Caemmerer and the Lutherans do not follow Saint Augustine in his employment of *caritas* and other concepts of earthly love as part of the drama of divine love or *agape,* I am always impressed by the degree to which they share his interest in dramatizing the radical disjunction between church and world or between the city of God and the city of man. An overlooked resource in relating the two might well be Augustine's concept of a *natura* operative in the city of man. Both the godly and the godless stand in relation to it; the godly or heir of the heavenly city sees *natura* transformed as part of the drama of salvation. The godless serves the purposes of God, perhaps without knowing it, through his proper use of this potentiality which God has put into the creation and given to men. Thus Augustine provides theologically for the apparent good of this world that does not belong to the city of God. Augustine employs a view of relative or limited goodness (*City of God, XIV,* 5—6; *XV,* 4, 22) which he sees in justice, righteous victory, peace, even female beauty and the flesh itself! Thus human virtue can be a model or improving example — as it practically is — for the citizens of the city of God (V, 18). It is evidenced in friendship, manners, and patriotism (XVIII, 41). There is no eternal salvation connected with this use of the created nature: "They have received their reward" in the virtues of civic benefits. Like Caemmerer, Augustine finally says that its virtues are but seeming virtues (and thus *absolutely* vice) because it lacks full recognition of the true God (XIX, 25). But even in Augustine's often-gloomy view this nature when properly used even in the city of the devil is good in itself (XV, 22). All this is a way of saying that while Augustine stresses the *fallen* creation, he will never let go of the idea theologically that it is God's fallen *creation.*

C. Luther's teaching of *justitia civilis* offers hopeful possibilities and plays a larger part in Caemmerer's oral tradition than it does in this soteriological context. In class he liked to remind us, for example, that an agnostic Jew like Joseph Pulitzer might, through his wars for civic virtue and against political exploitation, have done more in the service of God for the earthly city than did any number of Christian ministers. It seems to me that it would be fruitful to develop this theological concept as well as to use its practical consequence. *Justitia civilis* is not *die Gerechtigkeit die vor Gott gilt,* but it is a kind of righteousness which provides a clarified pattern of licit action for Christians who would work with worldlings and who would creatively interpret their joint work.

D. When the law of God is studied only *in loco justificationis* as Lutherans like to do *("Lex semper accusat;* the Law always accuses")*, the point is often overlooked that its accusing force is operative *in loco justificationis* only. Then men forget that the Law of God is the law *of God,* that it too is of His Word and will for man, that it is a *dynamis* or power — not unto salvation but unto civil righteousness and under the lordship of Christ in the world where one's neighbor stands in need and where one must be concerned and care-full in light of that need. Christians who neglect this Biblical motif are in danger (as Caemmerer is not, but as some of his students have seemed to be) of tending toward a Marcionitic view in which the Law seems almost to emanate from a lesser god or antigod.

IV

Looking back on the years of Caemmerer's participation in his church's evangelical and ecumenical awakenings in the light of a restudy of this his basic argument about the church, it seems incredible that he should ever have been accused of being a theological "liberal." If "liberal" means as it usually does that the theologian stresses as much as he can the continuities between nature and grace or nature and supernature, then *The Church in the World* and its author are profoundly illiberal. The label is unimportant but the argument behind it was. He permits no word in his book which in any way minimizes the drama of God's reconciling intervention in a fallen world. He restricts Christian participation in the world to evangelism or the preevangelical activities of witness or the postevangelical activities of service in order that more men might be saved. There is no talk of serving or understanding the world for its own sake or in its own light.

Never should the clarity of this evangelical doctrine be lost, muffled, or obscured. But in a church which finds it too easy to turn its back on human need and on the structures of daily life (and thus cutting them loose into unreflective secularism) we need also a rationale for positive relations to that world which does not, does not yet, or never may be led to explicit faith in Jesus Christ. The Biblical exegete must deal with the *pleroma* or fullness of Biblical witness, must try to interpret the full range of random data of human experience. He must affirm where there can be affirmation just as he must condemn where he is called to the act of condemnation.

Therefore if it is possible to consolidate gains and to grow in grace, it is possible to remind ourselves daily of the saving accent of *The Church in the World* as we relate its teaching to the doctrine of creation. Failure to do so leads to a church which can easily be introverted, can reduce salvation to slogans, can fail to produce a culture-for-Christian-community, can add to the scandal of the Gospel by forcing it to appear in a culturally implausible or absurd setting: in short to be "crabbed, inbent, selfishly concerned only for survival" (p. 88). We need the "interim ethic" for life among the unsaved of the world or among those who do not know that they are saved or whom they are serving.

Caemmerer's book expresses again and again the regret and the sorrow of the sensitive Christian for a fallen creation that does not know its truth, beauty, and goodness in God. I was surprised to note how mournful and tired it sounds from time to time (pp. 87—89), not remembering its author in that light at all. Only one who loves God and the church so much as he does can have a standard by which to measure the tragedy of fallenness — or be inspired to write a book on the strategy of rescue. Professor Caemmerer evidently conceives of his book as a document for the Christian underground which will be called upon when the church is again persecuted, as he is quite sure it will be (p. 87). If anything I have written about a newer cultural situation seems to suggest that I think we have moved "beyond Caemmerer" and the situation to which his book is addressed, I have given a false impression. I have spoken of other things but not of greater things. And if the church *really* becomes the church in the world, I have little doubt but that his manual of arms will inform and inspire us who live in an untested and fat church in an affluent society. We have not yet caught up with it or its author or the divine vision with which they would nurture us.

"From Creation to the Last Judgment God is at work toward the world in Jesus Christ."

CHAPTER 9

The Church on Mission

ROBERT T. HOEFERKAMP

Trite but true is the assertion that the worldwide mission of the Christian church has moved into an anguished, self-critical phase which the enthusiastic proponents of the "evangelization of the world in this generation" could not have foreseen or understood. The factors that have contributed to this agonizing reappraisal of missions are common knowledge and need not be recounted here. Suffice it to say that the newly emerging nations look upon traditional institutional Christian missions as tools of the imperialistic aggrandizement of the Western powers. A great deal of thought and energy is being directed toward the removal of odious visible symbols (the mission compound) and practical measures (the dependence of the younger churches upon the decisions made by mission boards in North America and Europe) which embody the old missionary "imperialism." It might be asked whether a proportionate amount of investigation into the theological or nontheological concept of missions that was the driving force behind the era of missionary imperialism would not be equally or more fruitful for the development of a new vision and a new stance in the worldwide missionary task of the church. Could it be that the old vision was at least in part the product of a false concept of the church and of mission? And could it be that a more Biblical view of church and mission might be not only more relevant to present-day needs but also more nearly true and thus productive of a new realism, a new courage, and a new hope that will revitalize the allegedly flagging missionary efforts of the churches? This essay, which attempts to spell out the accents which the Reformation rediscovered on the basis of Holy Scripture, is a tentative first step toward such a vision of church and mission.

I

Students of Dr. Caemmerer have learned to view the church as the people of God, the living body of Christ in this world. From the outset I want to make it clear that this is the church whose reality I know and experience and in whose service I stand. It is the people among whom God's saving activity in Christ has taken hold and borne fruit. The church lives by the preached Gospel and the administered sacraments, through which God conveys His victory in Christ to the whole body of the faithful. At the same time, the Gospel and the sacraments find their home and dwelling in the church, which in turn propels them out into the world. In this connection we recall Luther's confession in the Large Catechism that the church is "the mother that begets and bears every Christian through the Word of God." [1] At the same time we can recall another keen word of Luther: "Christ would be nothing at all if He had simply been born physically in His own person, and if He were not at the same time born spiritually in His body, which is the Church." [2] That is to say, the Gospel wells up in the church and flows forth from it; and what is the Gospel and its effect but Christ Himself, *Christus praedicatus,* His very presence and His gifts of forgiveness, life, and salvation?

On this view, the church is seen primarily in personal and dynamic terms, not sociological or institutional. But this does not mean that the church embodies a Gnostic disdain of the material and a Docetic yearning for the spiritual. God is the Creator of the material, He sent His Son into the flesh, and He continues to deal with men on the analogy of the incarnation. Because the Gospel and the sacraments, the "constitutive factors" of the church, are audible, tangible, and visible, because the people whom Christ calls and in whom He lives and works are real human beings of flesh and blood,

---

[1] LC, Creed, 42. *The Book of Concord: The Confessions of the Evangelical Lutheran Church,* trans. and ed. Theodore G. Tappert in collaboration with Jaroslav Pelikan, Robert H. Fischer, and Arthur C. Piepkorn (Philadelphia: Muhlenberg [Fortress] Press, 1959), p. 416. (Hereafter cited as Tappert.)

[2] *WA* 5, 549, 30 ff.; 551, 6 ff.; cited by Wilhelm Maurer, "Reformation und Mission," *Lutherisches Missionsjahrbuch für das Jahr 1963: Ihr Werdet Meine Zeugen Sein: Georg F. Vicedom zum 60. Geburtstag* (Nürnberg, 1963), p. 34.

and because the Gospel and the sacraments need to be spoken and administered by living men in some sort of continuity with the past, institutions do legitimately and necessarily arise and take shape as a part of the church. Thus the church is as empirical as are the people who make it up, as are the Gospel and the sacraments, and as are the structures which become necessary for their administration. The neutral observer sees in all of this a typical cross section of organized religion structured to perpetuate and propagate itself. But the eye of faith perceives in, with, and under the institutional activity the heartbeat of the living body of Christ.

Although some measure of institutional stability in the church is necessary, the real secret of the church's life is the dynamic surge of the Gospel. The church in its innermost self is ceaseless motion, because the new age in Christ invades and conquers the old age as a restless, powerful reality. It is the new age that gives to the Gospel and the sacraments the pulsating force which they possess. Thus the Gospel and the sacraments are always in motion, for it is the living God who is in motion through them, gathering in His train all who have been born again by water and the Word and constantly widening the sweep of His activity throughout the world. Wilhelm Loehe said it: "Die Mission ist nichts als die Eine Kirche Gottes *in ihrer Bewegung.*"[3] As the church never ceases in her movement, it is clear that her mission is not self-generated or self-propelled but that the source of motion and mission is God. It is really *missio Dei.* But the God of the incarnation continues to veil (and simultaneously reveal) Himself in human flesh. He uses men to fulfill His mission. Through the Gospel and the sacraments, spoken and administered by men, He carries out a constant sifting and upbuilding process among the people who are the church, constantly reaching out into unevangelized areas in their lives and bringing these under the sway of the new age. In turn He uses these people, as they are continually nourished and renewed by the Gospel, to witness to the might of the new age among those who are still enthralled by the powers of the old. In this way God energizes and uses His people to do His work of *missio.*

But the people of God need to structure and organize themselves in order to carry out this task. They may be dissatisfied with the

[3] Cited by Werner Elert, *Morphologie des Luthertums,* corrected reprint, I (Munich: C. H. Beck'sche Verlagsbuchhandlung, 1952), 340, trans. Walter A. Hansen, *The Structure of Lutheranism,* I (St. Louis: Concordia Publishing House, 1962), 390.

anachronistic structures inherited by them from the past; they may attempt to reform them or to create new structures that respond to the demands of the present era. But structures they are, and structures they remain: human, fallible, and subject to progressive abuse and decay. God may indeed raise up extraordinary prophets who scorn the institutions of the organized church and who strike out on new paths in order to perform the *missio Dei.* But these men end by establishing their own structural patterns, against which a new generation of Young Turks will inevitably rebel.

Thus in its heart and soul the mission of the church is no human enterprise that thrives on spinning the organizational wheels. It is rather the whole people of God testifying to the wisdom of God hidden in the folly of the cross and to the powers of God hidden in its weakness. But the people of God do require organizational structure in order to carry out the *missio,* and too often, apparently, the organization has to bear the brunt of the task. Here again the man on the street and the social scientist concur in their evaluation of mission as organized religious propaganda; and because we bearers of the mission are not only righteous but also still sinners, we need not deceive ourselves that some measure of organizational propaganda does not almost inevitably accompany the dynamic action of God the Holy Spirit as the mission is on the move. But the heartbeat of mission is always the Gospel power of God at work in the faithful, and this power is always sufficient to judge and renew the claims and pretensions of organizational structures which seek to make of themselves ends and not means.

II

In the main we agree with the now commonly accepted thesis that the church does not exist for itself but for the world. Of course, in the highest and holiest actions of the church, for example in supreme moments of communion with God through worship, it seems impertinent to put the question: "Does this act of worship become an end in itself, or does it serve some 'nobler' purpose?" We would venture the statement that the edification of the faithful and the glorification of God which occur in worship are proper ends in themselves. But it is also true that the faithful are edified for witness and service, and that God is glorified in order that the ends of the earth may see and praise His glory. Given the natural inclination of congregations and church bodies to make the maintenance of their own internal structure the object of their most earnest strivings, we think it perennially necessary to stress that the church exists for the world, in the sense that the church is God's instrument for communicating His salvation to the world which He created.

We are emerging from an era in which not a few pious Christians thought of the church and its mission in all-too-individualist terms. Missions were seen as the active concern of the pious, dedicated *kleine Herde* among the great mass of nominal Christians. These pious few prayed, sacrificed, and worked for the salvation of souls. These souls that were saved became, in turn, another island of a pious few who were antiseptically sealed off from the *massa perditionis* of the rest of humanity. These souls cut themselves off from the secular concerns of the civil community and gave their best efforts to rescuing as many more souls as would fit into the tight little island of the saved.

We are more and more coming to see that such a conception of missions is an indefensible abridgment of the full-orbed Biblical accents on church and mission. To be sure, we cannot overlook the incontrovertible Biblical emphasis on the individual person. Our Lord was interested not only in the crowds but sought out with loving concern the individuals who made up those crowds. The apostles were mightily concerned that salvation in Christ should reach the individual, be he Jew or Greek. However, always bearing in mind the need for individual repentance and faith, we feel that our times demand a recognition of the comprehensive Biblical view of the task of the church on mission. We mention three aspects of this Biblical view.[4]

First, mission is the church as the *entire* people of God (and not just a few select souls) witnessing and mediating to the "nations" God's Word of judgment and salvation in Jesus Christ. Indeed, individuals are added one by one to the church through repentance and faith. But this category of the individual does not exhaust the fullness of what the Scriptures say about the extent of God's salvation. Isaiah does not tire of praising the universal sweep of God's saving deeds: "The Lord has bared His holy arm before the eyes of all the nations, and all the ends of the earth shall see the salvation of our God" (52:10). It is impossible to escape the clear intent of St. Paul's state-

---

[4] I herewith acknowledge the stimulation I have received from the mimeographed study paper of Martin L. Kretzmann entitled "The Church Is Christ's Mission." This paper has been developed by Dr. Kretzmann as the theological basis for his recommendations as Mission Study Director to The Lutheran Church — Missouri Synod.

ments about the successive universal sway of the first and the Second
Adam over mankind (Rom. 5:12-21; 1 Cor. 15:21-22). "God was
in Christ reconciling the *world* to Himself" (2 Cor. 5:19). The seer
of the Apocalypse hears the loud voices in heaven saying: "The kingdom of the world has become the kingdom of our Lord and of His
Christ, and He shall reign forever and ever" (11:15). And in his
vision of the new Jerusalem the leaves of the tree of life "were for
the healing of the nations" (22:2). In the consummation of all
things, not only individuals but peoples and nations will enter the
kingdom of God; and this kingdom will not merely have as its object
the "heavenly" joys of the pious, but it will encompass a new heaven
and a new earth in which God will reign over a new humanity. "For
God has consigned all men to disobedience, that He may have mercy
upon all." (Rom. 11:32)

We do not mean to imply that the church is hereby given leave
to offer to the peoples of the world a kind of cheap grace that
would exclude the necessity of conversion. But we are concerned that
as God's dynamic impels the church onward in its witness to the
world, it dare not suppress these universal accents of the Gospel and
it dare not lose sight of itself as God's instrument through which, in
His own good time and by the power which He alone comprehends
and exercises, He desires to make "all" partakers of His salvation.

Second, the church on mission in its corporate life as the people
of God reflects the fullness of salvation which is for all nations and
all men. As the reestablishment of fellowship between sinful man
and the holy God, "salvation" is wholeness, completeness, fullness;
and it affects and embraces the whole life of the individual, of all
mankind, and of all the created world. The entire Bible mocks the
efforts of all who would restrict God's salvation to the private, pious
concerns of the soul and consign the body and the physical world to
the realm of the merely secular that is doomed to perish. Salvation
for the people of God in the Old Testament always included return
to and tenure of the Promised Land. When our Lord announced the
Good News of the inbreaking of the Kingdom, He preached, taught,
and healed the sick. Thus by anticipation He showed that the life
of the Kingdom is the life in which the disastrous split between flesh
and spirit has been overcome. The New Testament church is indeed
not a Platonic, imaginary state, but it is the very real "place" where
the sacraments are in use to nourish and activate the church for its

mission. As we are reminded in the Large Catechism, the sacraments convey to us salvation in body and soul and are the sure pledge that we shall rise to eternal life in body and soul.[5] In the sacraments God takes ordinary elements of the old creation and makes them vehicles of the gifts and powers of the new creation. Accordingly, we do not think it too far afield to conclude that through the sacraments God indicates that His salvation embraces already now all created life and that all created life will be re-created in the new heavens and the new earth.

All of this has important consequences, we think, for the mission of the church. It shows that the church is to concern itself not only with the soul but also with the body of man. It indicates that the church's message has pertinence not only for the private needs of the individual but also for the public and secular needs of the body politic. When the church and its servants direct their efforts to the whole man and his needs in medical, agricultural, educational, and welfare work, they witness to the truth that God the Redeemer is God the Creator and that the Triune God has redeemed all of life for all men. When the church speaks not only to the faithful within the four walls of the sanctuary but also lets its voice be heard in the public sphere, speaking out for social, economic, and racial justice and for understanding and reconciliation among the nations, it demonstrates in concrete fashion that the Triune God is the Lord of all life and that all of the life of man and the world is His sphere of action.

Third, mission is the church as the people of God witnessing in word and deed to the all-encompassing salvation of God, and doing this "in the form of a servant." The churches in the economically powerful countries of the world are coming to realize that, as they pursue their mission in the underdeveloped nations, they must dissociate themselves from the economic and political aims and ends of the countries in which they live. And this is not easy, since Christian faith is more intimately bound up in men's minds and souls with nationalism and economic, social, and political convictions than they generally realize. It is not easy, since it is the economic resources in which Christians who live in the advanced countries participate which enable them to carry out the mission in the underdeveloped nations. It is difficult for Christians who live in a country whose official ideol-

---

[5] LC, Baptism, 44—46; Lord's Supper, 68 (Tappert, pp. 442 and 454).

ogy is a kind of theology of glory to put into actual practice the theology of the cross. Yet the theology and practice of mission is the theology and practice of the cross, and it is to this theology and practice that Christians are being inexorably called in our contemporary world. The powers of the world of the resurrection are indeed at work in the present age, but they are hidden under the cross of Christ. Therefore Christians of the more advanced countries are called upon to relinquish their pretensions to superior knowledge, power, and sophistication and to share the love of Christ in word and deed with the less fortunate peoples of the world. When the church and her members do not boast that they possess the panacea for all the problems of mankind, but when they selflessly attack the perennial human problems in the name and the spirit of the Lord Jesus Christ, the true light does indeed dispel the darkness, and the new age puts to flight the powers of the old.

III

These lines are written against the background of 12 years of experience in the mission of the church in Central America. It would seem fitting and necessary to illustrate by concrete example from Central and Latin America what we have said about church and mission. While the question of the unity of the church is to be treated elsewhere in this volume, it is impossible to speak about the mission of the church in any area of the world without touching on the problem of Christian unity. The matter of Christian unity seems as urgent in Latin America as in any other part of the globe. The secularism that is the dominant force in what may variously be described as pre-, sub-, and post-Christian Latin America can only shrug off as ineffectual and irrelevant a divided Christian witness. Protestants are now 10 to 12 million strong in all of Latin America. The Pentecostal variety of Protestantism is growing at a quite rapid pace, but Protestant forces in general seem unable to make inroads among the potentially most influential sectors of the population: students, intellectuals, the managerial class, and industrial workers. On the other hand, the long-stagnant forces of Roman Catholicism are in many places awakening to the renewal that is spreading throughout the rest of the Roman Church. But in most cases the visible progress toward renewal is bound to be slow, and meantime the Roman Church finds that her witness is most ineffectual among virtually the same population groups that the Protestants find difficult to reach.

It seems that some semblance of unity in mind, spirit, and message is going to have to be achieved among the various Christian
groups before the Christian witness can effectively be conveyed to
a secularized public for whom Christian faith is superstition or a sentimental whim of the moment of a mere aesthetic thrill. And it
seems that before such a semblance of unity is achieved, a deepgoing
renewal will have to take place on all sides, *both* Protestant and
Roman Catholic. Latin American Protestants need not point their
finger only at hard-shell Roman Catholic intransigence and reaction,
for many Protestants likewise hide behind a well-nigh impenetrable
armor of prejudice, social and cultural backwardness, and fundamen-
talism of a type that is hopelessly out of contact with contemporary
life. If the "confessional mission" to which the writer has dedicated
his years of labor can help to soften up these rigidities on all sides,
and if the Holy Spirit wills to use this type of mission, with its central
emphasis on the Gospel and the sacraments, as a means toward the
renewal of all the church in Latin America, he believes that such
accomplishments are worthy missionary goals, even if they do not
always coincide with missionary aims as they are more conventionally
spelled out.

Any idea of the visible and organic reunion of all Christian
groups in Latin America in this or any immediate future generation
is, of course, out of the question, at least as far as we can humanly
see. But we can visualize within the foreseeable future the gradual
rapprochment of some or many Christian bodies, including certain
groups within the Roman Catholic Church. For example, even now
there are certain spirits within the Roman Church in Latin America
who realize that basically all Christian groups face the same difficulties
and are in the same basic situation as they strive to witness to the
heart and mind of a secularized world that fully realizes that the age
of ecclesiastical domination is past. Can we not hope, pray, and
work for some sort of consensus on the part of influential elements
within the major Christian groups in Latin America, Roman Catholic
and Protestant, regarding the nature of the world in which the mission
is to be accomplished and regarding the scope, aim, and methods
of the one mission of the one church? When in the following lines
we speak of the "church" in Latin America we mean the *Una sancta*
of the Creed as it comes to some sort of realization in some such
consensus.

Given the nature of the church itself, the type of Christian tradition that has taken root in Latin America during four centuries, and the mental and spiritual makeup of Latin Americans, the church that is renewed by Word and Sacrament will manifest a sacramental and liturgical fullness and wholeness that it does not now possess. At the same time it will be *tecta cruce,* hidden under the judgment of the cross. In this way it will seek to maintain in fruitful tension both Catholic substance and Protestant principle. As the living body of Christ, it will seek to overcome the false institutionalism of Rome and the false individualism of the Protestants. As the recipient of the power of Word and sacraments and as the medium of their communication, it will transmit to its members the dynamic of God's salvation and so equip them as bearers of the Gospel. It will strive to refashion and readapt the traditional ecclesiastical structures in order to meet the missionary exigencies of the hour. With its institutions thus streamlined for action and with the missionary consciousness thus throbbing throughout all its members, the church will share its witness, and thereby the saving presence of Christ, with all sorts and conditions of men, but in particular with those influential sectors of society to which we referred before.

As the church goes about its mission, it will be passionately aware of the social, economic, and political patterns of the countries in which it works, for it will live with its feet firmly planted on Latin American soil; and so it will refrain from imposing upon the national Christians the customs and culture of a sending body of Christians abroad. It will minister in the form of a servant. It will renounce all pretensions to temporal ecclesiastical power and privilege. It will not be bound to any ideology, be it capitalist or socialist. It will strive to make it difficult for men to interpret its mission as the beachhead for the cultural and spiritual invasion of a foreign power. The church will share the misery of the dispossessed, it will suffer with the undernourished and the sick, it will bear the burden of the hopeless and the outcast. It will serve with the *verlorene Liebe* of which the Reformer speaks, the love that knows that men will trample upon it, but which nevertheless continues to give and serve and offer itself for others. That is the nature of love, since it is the nature of the God who gives Himself to His lost creatures with a spontaneity that knows no end and a selflessness that asks for no reward.

"People's sacrificial love for one another is not just a pleasant by-product of Christianity, but the very purpose of the atonement."

CHAPTER 10

The Whole Church
as Servant

DAVID S. SCHULLER

A score of classes of theological students entered the Lutheran ministry remembering the familiar figure: fingers drawn together thumping the chest, face slightly strained as if peering through the class, and the refrain, "You've got t' *love* people." Two decades later the gesture and words still bring warm laughter from groups of pastors within the Missouri Synod. They are remembering "the prof" and one of his major motifs.

Prof. Richard R. Caemmerer spoke pastorally. He knew it and reminded his students of it. In this essay we will ponder some of the implications of "loving people" today.

The past 25 years have ushered in a day radically different from that of only a generation before. Fundamental continuities remain, but many have been strained as never before in the history of our culture. As a historian, Caemmerer would accent the continuities. As one interested in the contemporary social scene (where it still is difficult to be sure of perspective), permit me to emphasize the discontinuities. For there comes a time when change and distortion become so vast that the principles which guided generations of one's forebears no longer are adequate. Most of us unconsciously agree that principles do not change. A more careful examination suggests that there are "middle-range" principles which do change. A convincing argument can be made for the fact that as a people we are laboring under guiding concepts of the 18th-century Enlightenment which are totally inappropriate and ineffective today. We are confronted by the awesome need for "unlearning" as well as learning.

The seminal thinkers in a number of disciplines have called for a radical review of the presuppositions which guide their views and research. Economists are asked to reconsider the basic systems bequeathed them by the classical economists of the 18th century. Can the fundamental maxims regarding price, wages, and profits — some of which dominated technical and popular economic theories from the days of Adam Smith and David Ricardo — still be useful in a day in which the major presuppositions of the 18th century are no longer true? For example, the foundational concepts regarding wages all presuppose a condition of poverty in which workingmen must live just above the level of subsistence; this is the "normal" condition to which the economic order must return. All concepts developed from a root idea of scarcity. Until very recently most public and private programs within the United States still operated with these unquestioned 18th-century concepts. As the social and economic reality moved even further from the posited interpretations, the readjustments and qualifications necessary in using the old concepts became so great that the patches began to tear the old wineskins. But with what pain were the old wineskins given up! (For some the use of the old wineskin remains the touchstone to test one's orthodoxy and loyalty to all that is good, true, and beautiful.)

Similar patterns are evident in the political and social spheres. The social problems, the widespread confusion and disorder, the inability of either governmental or other agencies to cope with the difficulties and perplexities which are growing in severity are all symptoms, Lawrence Frank observes, of the growing obsolescence and increasing anachronisms in virtually every area of social life. The traditional beliefs and value systems that guided individual and corporate actions for the last two centuries are roughly challenged by the fact that those who attempt to utilize them are floundering dangerously. The 18th-century assumptions are no longer true. We need new formulations.

I would argue that the identical pattern is taking place within the church. Formulations and assumptions which were trustworthy in an earlier generation are spurious today. Professional and practical economists are not the only ones who fall in love with old wineskins! Many of the personal and institutional patterns through which we attempt to show love to people today are antiquated and sentimental. We are not quarreling with their intention nor with the goodwill of the individual Christian who utilizes a particular response as the channel through which his faith becomes active. Faithful leadership, however, demands a rigorous analysis of the old patterns to test their truth and adequacy for today. The church is asking for more than generalizations. Convinced that love must be demonstrated in service, very specific questions are being asked about the form that service should take. One does not long pursue the question before he is dealing with knotty problems regarding the role of the church over against other agencies, particularly governmental agencies. Perhaps the greatest barriers to effective service center about the role of the church in social action and in political decisions. No amount of pious talk can obscure the fact that a given decision regarding Social Security, housing for the aged, or ADC can affect more people (for good or evil) than can all Lutheran welfare work for the next century.

Thus it becomes clear that any definition of service — the diaconic work of the church — must be broad enough to include the spontaneous act of the individual as well as the organized program of a denomination. It must include the work of the layman, the interested amateur, and the professional; above all, it must include social action and education as well as direct welfare service. Since not all would agree that some of these are desirable or even legitimate expressions of service, we would suggest three fundamental questions that must be answered regarding the "shape" of the service of the church in this current decade.

(1) *Primary Goals.* How crucial is the diaconic work of the church? Our Lord was able to describe His entire ministry as *diakonia*. He was One moved by compassion. Many of His parables highlight the need for doing as well as hearing. The final judgment is portrayed as an examination of one's service. Disciples are admonished to be merciful; discipleship will be characterized by love. The early church believed that it was more blessed to give than to receive; its members sold their possessions for the community; the strong were to bear the infirmities of the weak. St. Paul portrays all of the work of God within man as culminating in self-offering service. Timothy is told that one who does not care for his own has denied the faith and is worse than an infidel. James, Peter, and John elaborate even more emphatically on the central theme of service.

Yet it has become possible for us to define the work of the church in such a way that this overpowering witness is lost. The evangelistic task of the church is unconsciously pitted against its diaconic work. It has followed that when the primary work of the church is seen as "saving souls" or — in a narrow sense — as "preaching the Gospel," then the service of the church is seen either as an illegitimate work or at best as secondary to other more necessary tasks.

(2) *Responsible Agent: Individual or Church?* We are not suggesting that some Christians seriously argue against acts of love and service. For a time, however, uncertainty arose regarding who is to carry out this work — the individual or the congregation as an organization. The traditional Lutheran view is strong in its insistence that the individual Christian is to function in the social and political realm. That this is also a function of the congregation was denied by some and affirmed by others. Some condemned the involvement of the congregation in social action or welfare as sectarian error; others looked upon such an involvement as active obedience to a divine mandate exemplified in the practice of love and service by the newly formed New Testament congregations.

As time went on, Lutherans in the U. S. A. particularly became increasingly aware that as organized groups too theirs was a divine mandate.

As a result there has been a strong and widespread upsurge in the time and energy devoted to welfare work. In The Lutheran Church — Missouri Synod it culminated in a synodical resolution by the Chicago convention (1947) to create a department of welfare to coordinate and promote welfare work throughout the land. And in 1950 this department began to function. During the 15 years of its life it has flourished beyond all expectations and made the membership of the Synod truly alive to its responsibilities and blessings.

(3) *Comprehensiveness of Scope.* Is *diakonia,* the activity of helpfulness which Christians render their fellowmen in the love of Christ, restricted to direct service? Or is it possible that to render the truest and most helpful service one also must be concerned with the indirect service which comes through the structures of society as a result of social education and action? If *diakonia* focuses on the need of the other — and seeks to minister to the greatest amount of need possible — is not the Christian under obligation to seek cor-

porate action for the alleviation of social ills? Diaconic service which is to face the realities of the latter half of the 20th century must utilize social welfare work which is directed toward the immediate physical and temporal needs of the individual; but it also must include social action which addresses itself to the underlying conditions that produce the situations of need. Perhaps at one time Christmas baskets were a useful device for conveying Christian helpfulness; today they are virtually obsolete and inappropriate. In our society the Christian who would show mercy must become involved with the tangled questions of justice and exploitation, employment and housing, which produce and perpetuate cases of poverty.

We shall find the three questions of goal, agent, and scope useful categories as we assay the need for diaconic work within the church today. One discerns a number of trends as he compares the service of the church a century ago with that of our day. Five of these impressions appear significant; at the same time they underscore points which need further emphasis in the immediate future.

First, the work of service has moved from a position of an admirable "extra" task of the church to where it is evaluated as a symptom of a church's vitality. The Lutheran Church has experienced periods where its emphasis on strict dogmatic definition was set in opposition to a rich life of faith and service. There have been times when she remained quiet in the face of appalling conditions of human need. Oddly enough, her rich heritage has been used to perpetuate this false dichotomy. Where, for example, the polemical nature of the Lutheran Confessions and their specific context were forgotten, later generations have been ill-equipped to do battle in a vastly changed situation. Thus the polemical quality of the articles of the Augsburg Confession on New Obedience, the Church, and Good Works has led a later generation of Christians to the point where the spontaneous expression of faith flowing into love was hampered.

In our day, however, the disparity between the affluence of the organizational church and the disadvantaged segments of the American population has forced the church to reexamine its own heart. The postwar temptation to flee areas of cities which were rapidly becoming blighted and our inability to make meaningful contact with vast segments of the population who differed from an older generation of Lutherans forced the church to take stock of its own goals. During the 1950s the change slowly took place. One denomination after another began to make loud confession as it rediscovered the inner city. A half generation of angry young clerics turned their backs on the suburban country clubs with stained-glass windows to become shepherds of the poor and the downtrodden.

"Servanthood" became the theme of their concern. Phil. 2 set the stage: The life of the Christian and of the church was to be a reenactment from below of the servant shape of Jesus Christ. They took the world seriously — far more seriously than had the church for many generations. They read Bonhoeffer and accepted his "world come of age." The more they faced the complexity of the urban scene and sensed their relative helplessness to effect basic change or to provide genuine help, the more intensely they moved into the posture of servants. Living increasingly "in the world," they came to know the pain, the struggle, the frustrations and aspirations of people. They longed with the heart of God to reach out with healing. They had little patience with the "religious enterprise." In most cases there was little left to preserve. But there were people to be served. For them diaconic service never again could become an "extra"; they have become our consciences . . . and our teachers.

Secondly, diaconic work has moved increasingly from being the province of special-interest groups within the church to being the task of the *whole* church. Strikingly the first part of this drama was played just over a century ago. The year 1848, when revolution rolled throughout Europe, marked the beginning of an awakening on the part of the evangelical church in northern Europe to the desperate needs of the masses. Until that time many private and individual efforts were made to serve those caught in various plights. Each was partial. None made a significant impact on the larger group. The middle of the 19th century, however, saw the rise of three men who left an indelible imprint on the shape of all Lutheran diaconic work. They were Johann Wichern (1808—81), Theodore Fliedner (1800—67), and Wilhelm Loehe (1808—72).

Heavily influenced by the theology of Schleiermacher, Wichern called the church of his day to repentance, insisting that love was its responsibility as much as faith. To move an institution that had lost touch with the common life of people in the working classes, he utilized the flexibility of voluntary societies outside the official church. Lay activity was prominent; he worked heavily in the area of education. When the revolution came, Wichern saw it as the church's great opportunity to launch a full-scale mission to the whole of society. It was due primarily to his efforts that the Inner Mission work became nationwide in Germany.

Similarly, Fliedner began the training of deaconesses; through his efforts women were channeled into effective service in hospitals and elsewhere. Nurses, teachers, and social workers came from the deaconess motherhouse. But with Fliedner the work remained voluntary. Highly effective leavening was the result. But it appeared to be an effort that ran parallel to the work of the church itself.

Of the three men, Loehe did most to root these vital efforts in the life of the church itself. He feared that the life and order of the church were endangered by these parachurch activities. To keep diaconic work closer to the patterns of the New Testament, he insisted that this had to become once again the work of the whole church, under its supervision and supported by its efforts. In Loehe we find the wedding between mission responsibility and social responsibility. With his accent on ecclesiology, Loehe worked to reshape the work of service within a Lutheran matrix of doctrine, worship, and life.

Sadly, later generations relived the mistakes of the official church of an earlier period before breaking through again to conclusions strikingly similar to Loehe's. After a century in which voluntary associations, apart from the church's main structure, dominated the church welfare scene — serving retarded children, establishing hospitals, forming children's homes and homes for the aged — signs on the horizon again are indicating that the church itself feels that these expressions of service are an intrinsic part of her work. As an exploratory study phrased it, this marks the transition of *diakonia* from an "option" of a society to an "office" of the church.

One need not be a cynic to recognize that this marks an advance but also poses new dangers. The church recognizes her inevitable responsibility; but as she assumes control, this places the work in the context of larger bureaucracy. As Berger had demonstrated, the longer church welfare work proceeds in a professional manner under bureaucratic control, the more it resembles the work conducted under secular auspices. The spontaneous response of faith creatively seeking new avenues for love to meet human need is smothered beneath the necessary weight of bureaucratic structure. The individual's personal response to neighborly need inevitably changes to response to a cleverly designed memo from the public relations office of the local district of the denominational welfare department. On the one hand this means that Christians are responding with aid to crisis on the other side of the globe. Negatively it often amounts to weighing one more appeal of some 3 dozen which come to the average family in the course of a year. Special appeals must become part of an ongoing budget if need is to continue to be met. Routine replaces spontaneity, agencies replace individuals, professionals replace amateurs, budget replaces free gifts. But at this juncture in history, these have become the channels through which faith active in love must flow to perform a global task.

In the third place, the service of the church must continue its movement from exclusive concern with *ad hoc* cases of need to the more primary level of prevention. In the past when sickness, fire, or flood struck, the Christian community moved in with personal help. Now we have become aware that certain types of need have developed their own culture. Such a culture is impervious to the isolated effort of goodwill; it needs study and analysis, experimental approach of task forces to test methods, and then the concerted efforts of vast numbers to effect changes in values, attitudes, and behavior of whole subpopulations within a society.

Consider the goal of rehabilitation of those in the "welfare class." Men like Robert D. Hess have extended the thesis that poverty in our country has become a culture and a way of life for some groups and that this way of life is taught to the next generation. This is to say that economic, social, and educational poverty is socialized in early childhood. Hess argues effectively that our present policy of dealing with poverty does not eliminate it but institutionalizes it and thus is in the process of creating a permanent welfare class. A rapid survey of most service efforts for this group — both within and outside the church — indicates that they have been directed primarily to the consequences of this culture of poverty rather than to its basic causes. Consider the programs developed to deal with unwed mothers, children from broken homes, delinquents, school dropouts, illiterates, alcoholics, and parolees.

When the church attempts to work on a more basic level, it will be forced to sharpen the definition of its own role. For scores of other agencies — private, state, and federal — are at work on the now-popular "poverty program." In the past we frequently ran programs in competition with or at least parallel to those of other groups. Because of the vastness of the need, coordination is necessary as never before. The very recognition that the concern of the church is with the whole of life has thrust us into many strange battlefields — standing side by side with even stranger fighting comrades. At times churchmen react aggressively to the awareness that other groups are attempting to serve. How strange that the church should want to restrict service to its own halfhearted efforts! Nygren said long ago that the church should be grateful for what the state and other agencies have been able to do — but this does not relieve the church of its responsibility, "because to serve is part of the church's nature." The church remains the institution which might maintain the motivation, the structure, the flexibility, and the judgment to serve in a totally unique fashion. Where others restrict their attention to only one problem or age group, the church could address its efforts to integrating service once again. There are many areas of need at the present time which "fall between" the efforts of other groups. Some in need fail to meet the qualifications set in order to be helped by other agencies. The diaconic ministry of the church is ideally suited for reaching out in mercy to such people.

The fourth change has seen the first movement within the Lutheran Church from an exclusive concern with welfare work to the additional battlefronts of social education and action. When one becomes seriously involved in helping those submerged at the lowest level of the social, educational, economic, and political scale, he is forced to the conclusion that any help designed to be more than a gesture of goodwill must deal with the underlying conditions which suppress continuing generations of people. There is an unbroken chain of inferior health, inferior education, inferior or nonexistent employment, inferior housing, and an inferior political voice. The walls out of the pit appear unscalable. A few escape. We sagely judge them to be the inwardly mobile ones who have caught the vision of another way of life and doggedly pursued it in the face of staggering odds. But the great mass of children born "at the bottom of the pack" are destined to spend their entire lives there. The vicious cycle must be broken at an initial point. Because the chain usually includes self-defeating images of self, a lack of available models representing another mode of life, and an ultimate resignation to one's lot, the impetus for change usually must come from the outside.

Where a church truly has stood with all of its people — including those at the bottom — it finds itself fighting for them. Indignation is felt when housing inspectors are instructed to overlook violations in the midst of hard-core slums, when narcotic traffic reaches out to another youngster in the parish, when 15-year-old girls are drawn into buying their piece of life and paying for it with their own bodies, when the boy who has caught the vision of the body of Christ is rounded up indiscriminately with the others simply because of his race, when 17-year-olds with good school records still read like 4th-graders, when defeat is seen in the eyes of the young dropout for whom no job ever is going to open. Indignation must move into action. In each case the problem is basically bigger than any difficulty which can be solved by a single individual. Structures and institutions within society are perpetuating patterns of exploitation.

Unhappily, it was not the church which called us to an awareness of these problems a decade ago. Those who did were segments of what we dismiss as the "world." But it was showing a compassion and a desire to fight for justice which should have characterized Christians. They took seriously these people caught in hard-core poverty. They were not condescending, sentimental, or paternalistic. In brutally realistic fashion they saw how those who had "arrived" in our industrialized-urbanized culture were able to protect themselves politically and make sure that their concerns were safeguarded. Those at the bottom were politically voiceless; they could not even make effective demands for such rudimentary city services as having their streets swept and repaired. Those who were concerned went to the voiceless and attempted to give them a voice and a new awareness of their potential power. They worked patiently in convincing people of the value of joining together with other voiceless people. In organization they possessed a power which they could never have as individuals. Thus community organizations began to develop across America.

Individual congregations discovered that these groups were helping people. At times their tactics seemed so raw, their motivations so dependent on hatred of the advantaged group, that the churches asked whether they could place their blessings on some organizations and certain approaches. Churches found themselves out in the streets where decisions were far more difficult, where motivations were mixed, but where life was being lived! Some congregations hesitated; others plunged into full cooperation with community organizations. Still others sought to define their relationship by acting responsibly as each new decision had to be faced — and yet consciously tried to remain the church. One Lutheran pastor who has walked the path of complete service to his people in a depressed area of New York said recently: "If our parishes are to be renewed, we must love the world before we love the church." We are discovering that love of the world must be translated into specific action, or it remains a lofty profession which mocks our lowly practice.

Finally, the tragic bifurcation between theology and life, liturgy and action has been bridged. The emerging pattern of diaconic work grows from a conscious theology and is nourished by a rich sacramental life of worship. Perhaps some representing an earlier generation of Lutheran pastors in this country turned in frustration from a theology which seemed sterile in producing compassion. But their work has suffered from a theology which has been too thin to support patterns of service adequate for our day. Their sons follow with a much richer theology. They are consciously churchmen. They find worship central in their personal and vocational lives. Their finest examples are confessionally Lutheran and yet catholic in their outlook. They are able to enter into dialog with Roman Catholic as well as with Protestant. Moreover they can discuss theology as well as practical programs.

These men are convinced that the greatest need for the church to perform her ministry of service more effectively lies not in new techniques, programs, or even insights. They are calling for a new look at the Gospel; the renewal must be a theological renewal. One of the most significant addresses I have heard within the last year was delivered by an Episcopalian priest deeply involved with the life of the inner city of Boston. The entire address was a cogently argued *theological* treatment of the work of the church in the city. He began simply: "Jesus Christ. In these two words all of human life is summed up — the life that the church lives for the sake of the world, and the life that the world lives for the sake of the church." He began with the fact of the death and resurrection of our incarnated Lord, with the peace that this has established among all men. Relentlessly he pursued the implications into the facets of the misshapen life of the church and the broken lives of those in the city. He called the church, which has become so ecclesiocentric that she has grown blind to the deepest needs of society, back to theology and worship: The church at worship is the church learning in each age what it means to serve and to be served by humanity.

Many factors have driven the church back to an awareness of

her need to serve. Regardless of the initial impulse, this service will remain partial and will be subject to being untrue to the nature of the church unless it is nourished and corrected by the Word of God. Concern lies in two directions. First, every generation must be aware of apostasy. I strongly suspect that some men are entering the service professions — within or outside the church — because their faith is bankrupt. Not sure of God, too overpowered by doubt to proclaim the Gospel, they do not take the radical leap of leaving the church. Many remain within the ranks of the clergy, but their approach henceforth has little relationship to that of the apostle who "determined not to know anything among you save Jesus Christ, and Him crucified."

Furthermore, the renewal within theology is enabling us to avoid the tragic separation between renewal and creativity in program over against a rich, fermenting theological basis. Without this source, many of our most thrilling "service projects" today will be seen by future generations as but another manifestation of desperate techniques and despairing schemes of a floundering church.

The theology, teaching, and ministry of our mentor would enthusiastically undergird most of these trends which we have described as desirable. That service be more than an ecclesiastical extra, that it become the task of the whole church, that it move to a deeper level of prevention, that it become even more consciously theological and related to the life of worship — with these he would be in wholehearted agreement. Regarding the agent of service and change, his accent as preacher has been on the service of the Spirit-filled individual — who with his brothers in Christ compose the church. The generation of his students must test whether "to love people" today will not necessitate some secular forms of the church and social and political actions which would have seemed alien to an earlier generation of Lutherans.

"The agonizing quest for procedure and good conscience in matters of 'fellowship' speeded the study."

CHAPTER 11

On Developing
an Ecumenical Mind

Ecumenism as Renewal

RICHARD E. KOENIG

The 20th century, as has often been remarked, will enter the annals of Christendom as the century of the church. During the great era of missionary expansion the church raised the cross in many places where it had not been before, but in spite of this glorious chapter in Christian history the church remained divided. About the year 1900 something new entered the life of the church. After centuries of divisions and internal suspicion, Christians attained a fresh and reforming understanding of the church as the people of God and the body of Christ. Out of that understanding emerged the ecumenical movement, a worldwide impulse driving the churches closer together with a view to eventual reunion. The 19th century had as its goal the evangelization of the world; its dynamism created a revolution in the church which still continues.

The word "ecumenical" has a long history, dating back to the creed-making era of the church's history. Because *oikoumene* in Greek means "the inhabited earth," *ecumenical* was used by Protestant church leaders at the great missionary conference which convened in New York City in the year 1900 because "the plan of the campaign which it proposes covers the whole area of the inhabited globe." [1] Later, in 1925, another great conference convened in Stock-

[1] Quoted in John Mackay, *Ecumenics: The Science of the Church Universal* (Englewood Cliffs, N. J.: Prentice-Hall, Inc., 1964), p. 6.

holm, Sweden, called "The Universal Christian Council for Life and Work." This was translated into French as *Conseil Oecuménique du Christianisme Pratique* and into German as *Ökumenischer Rat für praktisches Christentum*. After Stockholm the word spread into common use in English as well as French and German as meaning "international in the sphere of church relations." [2] Its use was reinforced by the famous utterance of Archbishop William Temple shortly after the Oxford Conference of 1937, "The Ecumenical Movement is the great new fact of our time."

It is inevitable that a phenomenon so closely related to the life and welfare of the church should be treated in a volume dedicated to Richard R. Caemmerer. Few theologians have kept the church so steadily in view throughout their work. His volume *The Church in the World* leads out from the statement:

> The men of God in Christ are the church of God and the church of Christ. They are not, however, merely a collection of individuals. The church is not an abstraction or a title for all individual Christians. The church is a fellowship and a body; the fellowship of Christ and the body of Christ. Because of this fact the individuals of the church are more than what they are alone and individually; and the church is more than the sum total of individuals.[3]

"The church is not an abstraction"; it consists of "men of God in Christ." The passage breathes the spirit of ecumenism and urges us to consider one of the problem areas in that movement — the devlopment of what we shall call the ecumenical mind.

I

At "mid-career" in the quest for Christian unity it is difficult for second- and third-generation post-Edinburgh Christians to appreciate what a wonder the ecumenical movement in fact is. Ecumenical personalities make the front cover of weekly newsmagazines, and the assemblies of the churches are widely reported. Whether the traditional procession of robed clergy or the press conferences of influential and powerful churchmen hold our attention or not, we have all come to the point where we take such encounters and exposures for granted. It is easily forgotten how gingerly the churches approached one another in the early days of Faith and Order and Life and Work, how desper-

2 Leonard Hodgson, *The Ecumenical Movement* (Sewanee, Tenn.: The University Press, 1951), p. 5.

3 Richard R. Caemmerer, *The Church in the World* (St. Louis: Concordia Publishing House, 1949), p. 8.

ately they sought assurances that their trust in each other would not be abused. Without realizing it, the Christian churches by and large have come to assume what Angus Dun calls "the most elementary level of church unity . . . the unity of mutual recognition." [4] Most of the churches have chosen to express unity of mutual recognition by holding membership in the World Council of Churches. Others, such as the writer's own, have not done so, but the same church has made manifest its recognition of other churches in a variety of other ways, including the sending of official observers to the assemblies of the World Council.

Paradoxically the attainment of the present level of unity has created problems for the movement to reunite the churches. Having succeeded in drawing the churches out of their isolation and into conversation with one another, the ecumenical movement is in danger of stalling.[5] What was once a rushing, mighty wind threatens to become a zephyr blowing only gently through institutions which have risen up in response to the movement's pressures. The creation of councils of churches and what are known as "world confessional bodies" comes precariously close to letting the churches have their cake and eat it too. No one loses anything by joining one of the ecumenical organizations, since these bodies scrupulously avoid any abridgment of sovereignty or violation of member churches' convictions.[6] At the same time membership in such organizations enables a church to flatter itself on being ecumenical. To many people ecumenism has become synonymous with belonging to the World Council of Churches or some other world organization.[7]

It cannot be said forcefully enough that ecumenism is not exhausted or fulfilled by organizational membership. As originally con-

[4] Angus Dun, "The Purpose and Spirit of the Conference," *The Nature of the Unity We Seek: Official Report of the North American Conference on Faith and Order,* ed. Paul S. Minear (St. Louis: The Bethany Press, 1958), p. 39.

[5] Keith Bridston and Walter Wagoner, eds., *Unity in Mid-Career* (New York: The Macmillan Company, 1963), p. 3.

[6] Cf. "The Church, the Churches and the World Council of Churches," a statement received by the Central Committee of the World Council of Churches at Toronto in 1950, *Evanston to New Delhi* (Geneva: The World Council of Churches, 1961), pp. 245 ff.

[7] How much the contemporary confusion about the nature of the Christian church affects the ecumenical enterprise is problematical. Certainly the kind of debate that went on in Section I at the Fourth World Conference on Faith and Order, Montreal, 1963, points to another source of difficulty for the ecumenical movement. Theological disagreement would serve to make contentment with the *status quo* even more tempting.

ceived, the ecumenical movement meant the vision of the one church of Jesus Christ visibly gathered together to fulfill its one calling. The movement initially had little to do with organizations of any kind. It began from a *new type of interest* on the part of the churches in one another, as Hodgson states so well.[8] Under the impact of the movement churches previously hostile or unconcerned about one another began to see themselves and each other in a new light as part of one church, facing their common tasks together. The movement sprang out of a new mentality, an ecumenical mind, given to those who felt the burden of the church's mission. Ecumenism, therefore, is a spiritual event which implies renewal and a change of heart. Churches can cooperate without being changed, but this is not the fulfillment of the ecumenical vision.

In a sermon preached at the North American Conference on Faith and Order held at Oberlin, Ohio, in 1957 Visser 't Hooft argues that the ecumenical vision is no wild utopianism but grows out of and encloses a basic Biblical insight. Using as his text, "Therefore, holy brethren, who share in a heavenly call, consider Jesus, the apostle and high priest of our confession" (Heb. 3:1), he says:

> We are partners in that we have heard one and the same comprehensive call. What you have heard and what I have heard comes from one and the same God who speaks to us in one and the same man, Jesus Christ. We have one and the same hope of our calling — the hope for one and the same kingdom. If God's call to us is one call, that must mean that God sees us as one people, one family. We may draw as many dividing lines as we can, we may organize specific confessions and denominations; in God's sight there is just the one body of those who have heard his call and respond to it. God's Church cannot be divided because its unity belongs to its very essence. It has been remarked that in the impressive, monotonous enumeration in Ephesians 4: one body, one Spirit, one hope, one faith, one baptism, one Lord — we do not find the expression: one Church. The reason is surely that the oneness of the Church is so obvious to the New Testament generation that it need not be explicitly stated.[9]

He then concludes with the statement: "If we are really partners in one and the same call, unity — visible, convincing unity — is not a matter that Christians can be for or against. . . . This is part of our Christian commitment."[10]

8 Hodgson, p. 45.

9 Visser 't Hooft, "The Ground of Our Unity," Minear, pp. 122—24.

10 Ibid., pp. 123—24.

If ecumenism is a spiritual event, it is not an enterprise which can be confined to high-ranking churchmen who pursue it as a kind of hobby. We are not ecumenical only at the times when we are discussing church union. Ecumenism means *church* renewal. The ecumenical vision embraces the *total* Christian community, the whole people of God. Laymen and clergy alike are called to share and implement the dream of a Christian church which rises above its fragmented condition and tends toward the wholeness which is its destiny in Jesus Christ on every level. It is for that reason that the great ecumenical assemblies have emphasized the inclusion of the laity in the ecumenical task.[11]

Writes James Kennedy following the Third Assembly of the World Council of Churches in New Delhi in 1961: "The church cannot effectively be the church unless its members see themselves in their true light, that is, as members of the one body of Christ in the world. . . . No matter how many world gatherings of a few top ecumenical leaders are held, the vitality of all ecumenical activity and oneness in Christ depends on the lives of individual men and women for whom 'the Light of the world' is the light of their hearts and souls in everyday life and obedience." [12]

The emphasis within Protestant circles on ecumenism as inclusive of the whole people of God has received a surprising second in the decree *On Ecumenism* promulgated by the Second Vatican Council. The decree stated: "The attaintment of union is the concern of the whole church, faithful and clergy alike. This concern extends to everyone, whatever his talent, whether it be exercised in his daily Christian life or in his theological and historical research. This concern itself already reveals to some extent the bond of brotherhood between all Christians and it helps toward that full and perfect unity

[11] Cf. the Report of the Department on the Laity, in *Evanston to New Delhi*, p. 79. Also, Report of Section 5: "The Life of the Congregation," Minear, p. 217. Also the statement adopted by the World Council of Churches at New Delhi as quoted in *New Delhi Speaks* (SCM Press, 1962), p. 55: "We believe that the unity which is both God's will and his gift to his Church is being made visible as all in each place who are baptized into Jesus Christ and confess him as Lord and Savior are brought by the Holy Spirit into one fully committed fellowship, holding the one apostolic faith, preaching the one Gospel, breaking the one bread, joining in common prayer, and having a corporate life reaching out in witness and service to all, and who at the same time are united with the whole Christian fellowship in all places and all ages in such wise that ministry and members are accepted by all, and that all can act and speak together as occasion requires for the tasks to which God calls his people."

[12] James Kennedy, *No Darkness at All* (St. Louis: The Bethany Press, 1962), pp. 56—57.

which God in his kindness wills." [13] The decree went on to spell out the ways in which the Roman Catholic faithful are permitted and encouraged to express their ecumenical concern. Great emphasis was placed on prayer in common with other Catholics and, in certain special circumstances, with the "separated brethren." "Such prayers," read the decree, "are certainly an effective means of obtaining the grace of unity, and they are a true expression of the ties which still bind Catholics to their separated brethren." The point was made with Matt. 18:20 serving as the Biblical basis.

The Roman Catholic high regard for prayer as a means to unity and its commendation to the faithful form an exact parallel to a beautiful resolution of the World Council's Second Assembly at Evanston in 1954: "The measure of our concern for unity is the degree to which we pray for it. We cannot expect God to give us unity unless we prepare ourselves to receive his gift by costly and purifying prayer. To pray *together* is to be drawn together. We urge, wherever possible, the observance of the Week of Prayer for Christian Unity, January 18—25 . . . as a public testimony to prayer as the road to unity." [14] The two great branches of Christendom are one in their estimate of the people's prayer as "the soul of the whole ecumenical movement."

II

Hardly had the bishops completed their work and gone home from the third session of Vatican II when some Roman Catholic laymen began to carry out their church's decree *On Ecumenism*. At Amherst College two young faculty members initiated daily common prayer for Catholics and Protestants in the college chapel. Elsewhere, other Roman Catholic laymen sought different contacts with their "separated brethren." It appears that a genuine ecumenical enthusiasm exists within at least a portion of the Catholic laity. But, as one Catholic laywoman, a member of the Grail movement, asked, "Where are the Protestant laymen?"

Where, indeed? While instances of Roman Catholic lay concern for ecumenism continue to multiply, it is difficult to find an equal number of parallels among Protestants. For years there have been

---

[13] "Text of the Decree on Ecumenism Adopted by Bishops and Proclaimed by Pope," the New York *Times,* Sunday, Nov. 22, 1964.

[14] Quoted in Maurice Villain, *Unity — a History and Some Reflections* (Baltimore: Helicon Press, 1963), p. 67.

complaints that the ecumenical movement has not penetrated to the so-called grass roots. The florid words of Bishop Johannes Lilje that "a burning desire for greater Christian unity has spread and is spreading throughout Christendom like an irresistible, all-consuming prairie fire" [15] apply more in hope than in fact to the average Protestant congregation and church member. Where could one find, say, Lutheran laymen trying to arrange a service of common prayer with their Episcopalian neighbors? The week of prayer for Christian unity which Evanston recommended to the churches is one of the most difficult assignments faced by the local ministerial alliance and the individual pastor. "They won't come out," is the usual forecast, and "they" aren't the only ones. The attitude of the clergy, too, is something which is frequently less than a "burning desire for unity." As Martin Marty says, "The ecumenical movement hasn't caught on." [16]

There have been a number of theories advanced to explain the disturbing gap that often exists between the ecumenical ideal and its grass roots reception. One of the explanations says that the ecumenical vision suffers from a lack of concrete structures and symbols which would commend it to the attention of Christian people. "Where these symbols and structures of unity are absent — as they have been in the divided church — any powerful sense of community is inevitably absent too." [17] Others have seen the problem differently. In one of the more extended treatments of the subject, Martin Marty writes: "At the root of the problem may well be the fact that most people today are not, in any formal sense, theologically curious. Many do not ask the profound questions of life in a religious way and many who are religious do not ask them in a theological way. Perhaps part of the problem resides in what the ecumenical movement theologizes about." [18] Marty goes on to suggest that Christian people be engaged

[15] Johannes Lilje, "The Significance of the Ecumenical Movement," Minear, p. 127.

[16] It is astonishing that Faith and Order at Montreal in 1963 did not address itself to this question, especially in Section V, where "All in Each Place" was considered. Section I, which discussed the theme "The Church in the Purpose of God," also seems to have bypassed this crucial issue. Ecumenical lethargy is an ecumenical fact of grave importance, affecting the relationship of the churches to one another as much as some of the external pressures noted in Section I's report. (Cf. *The Fourth World Conference on Faith and Order* [New York: Association Press, 1964], p. 47.)

[17] Quoted in George Hunt, *A Guide to Christian Unity* (St. Louis: The Bethany Press, 1958), p. 89.

[18] Martin E. Marty, *Church Unity and Church Mission* (Grand Rapids: Wm. B. Eerdmans Publishing Company, 1964), p. 28.

in the ecumenical enterprise through mission, since this was the origin of the movement in the first place. Renewed mission will further the movement to unity and save it from premature aging.

Both of these suggestions are valuable, and both should be acted upon. But they suffer from a certain distance from what the ecumenical movement essentially is — the renewal of the church, the development of an ecumenical mind in which the churches see themselves as part of the one church. The lassitude with regard to ecumenism which is present in so much of the church is nothing less than evidence for the necessity of renewal. This is no tautology, for in order to effect some cure, we must understand the problem in its most radical dimension. What is needed for the ecumenical movement to catch on, for the ecumenical mind to take hold, is nothing less than a revival.

But revivals are notoriously difficult to induce, which is as it should be, since revivals, or renewals, belong to God and not to men. No techniques, no stratagems, no slogans, no campaigns, no matter how well intended or well thought out, will suffice to substitute for the Spirit who blows when and where He wills. Just as little as man can create the unity of the church, so little can he create the desire for unity, one aspect of what we have been calling the ecumenical mind. But God's activity never exempts man from his responsibilities. From the human point of view the development of an ecumenical mind for the church is both a call to prayer on the part of all those who feel the burden of a divided church and a summons to activity. But where shall we begin? A useful suggestion is found in Robert S. Bilheimer's fine book, *The Quest for Christian Unity*. He says:

> On every hand one hears the complaint that the ecumenical concept of the church is not living at the "grass roots." What is the real problem? It may be stated in some such fashion as this: That a concept of the church is being evolved in the ecumenical movement which is not the same as the concept which animates most of the denominations, and that the task is to modify the one by the other. The churches in general simply *have not had* a concept of unity which carried any power. . . . Our problem is to lodge a different concept of the church, namely, a truly ecumenical concept of the church, in each of the churches, with power.[19]

Earlier Bilheimer had spoken about the distinction between a working concept of the church and a theoretical concept of it. If the ecumeni-

[19] New York: Association Press, 1952, p. 108.

cal enterprise is to go forward, the theoretical, i. e., Biblical, concept of the church, the church as the body of Christ, must inform the church's life at every point.

There are many evidences that the churches already display a latent awareness of their presence in the one church of Jesus Christ. We refer to such commonplace activities as hymn singing and fund raising. All hymnals are radically ecumenical in character, and there is no exclusively denominational approach to stewardship. Fund-raising helps, one is inclined to say, are shared almost too readily by the churches. A more important piece of evidence for a latent ecumenical mind in the churches is their official disavowal of proselytism — the attempt to manipulate conversions by using the membership of other churches as a prospect list and mission field. About this Marty says: "Desisting from proselytism has a logical and a psychological corollary. If I do not enter a man's home and engage in proving to him that he is 'unsaved' . . . unless he breaks relations with his own church, I am asserting something positive. For if I have committed myself to the hope that salvation is in Jesus Christ and His truth, then — if I love my neighbor — I should make my view of truth prevail over alternative ones which he holds in Christ's name. If I do not, then I am suggesting that he is really 'saved.' " [20] Finally, there is the fact that most Protestant congregations in America have large numbers of people who have come to them from other denominations. Were it not for the interest and desire created by the churches from which they came, few Protestant congregations could have induced them to join their fellowship. The churches literally live from one another, especially in areas of transient population. (We shall have more to say about ecclesiastical symbiosis later on.)

Despite the elements which press for an open expression of the ecumenical mind, the churches frequently think and act in exclusive and autonomous terms. What needs to be done is to identify the places where the churches are manifesting an awareness of the one church and bring these to the attention of all. The more we can find elements to testify to our oneness and interdependence in Christ, the more the ecumenical mind will be reinforced. Conversely, the more clearly we can identify the ways by which our oneness is contradicted to the hurt of the church's mission, the more a desire for wider unity will be created. If a vision of the one church is spelled out in concrete

[20] Marty, pp. 35—36.

terms at all possible occasions, we can expect Christians to respond with devotion.

With devotion, not necessarily enthusiasm. The ecumenical movement is not quite the same thing as the missionary movement of the 19th century. Ecumenism means church renewal. The appropriate response to renewal is devotion. The missionary movement was more quantitative, a movement of expansion which lent itself to hanging maps and measuring advance by colored pins. The ecumenical movement is not so easily charted. It is a campaign of inner growth, a qualitative enterprise. It already has its songs. Is there a church which does not sing

> We are not divided,
> All one body we,
> One in hope and doctrine,
> One in charity?

The continual challenge is to sing the songs in a new way, with mind and heart attuned to the reality of the one church of Jesus Christ.

III

There is something to the dictum of Vatican II that ecumenism must be engaged in according to one's talent. No one would exempt or fence off the laity from any activity which would serve to create an ecumenical consciousness in the whole of the body, but realism bids us recognize such a task will have to be fulfilled by those whose calling it is to care for the churches. It is here that a serious sticking point appears.

The church, as Luther saw with characteristic clarity,[21] is a wholly worldly thing. In modern terms this means that the church has to be seen as an institution existing in the world like any other institution. It is a central feature of all earthly institutions, as it is of the human beings who create them, to avoid any possible threat to their existence. From a sociological point of view ecumenism is a threat to the church. The logic of a commitment to the idea of one church places a question mark over the church's continued existence as separate historical institutions. New Delhi heard Bishop Oliver Tomkins of Bristol say: "The achievement of unity will involve

---

[21] Cf. Franz Lau, *"Äusserliche Ordnung" und "weltlich Ding" in Luthers Theologie* (Leipzig, 1932). For the documentation I am indebted to Prof. Jaroslav Pelikan of Yale University Divinity School.

nothing less than a death and rebirth of many forms of church life as we have known them. We believe that nothing less costly can finally suffice." [22] Such talk does little to soothe those who sense ecumenism's threat to institutional stability or permanence. It would appear to be expecting too much for those imbedded in ecclesiastical institutions, which the churches really are, to recognize and implement the ecumenical vision.

Perceiving what a problem institutionalism poses for the attainment of unity, Faith and Order in 1955 decided to ask Dean Walter Muelder and Prof. Nils Ehrenstrom to head a special study commission to investigate the subject.[23] The approach was chiefly sociological and yielded some illuminating results. But, as Bilheimer insists, the task of acting upon the ecumenical vision is chiefly one for Christian faith. "Churches," he says, "are never merely sociological phenomena. They are basically rooms in the total household of faith. The question therefore is: Can the content of the gospel be so conceived and lived within these institutions to make them true to their basic character and genius? Can wisdom, freshness of approach, courage, and faith be so combined as to make this possible?" [24] Who dares say No?

Up to the present time an effective commitment to the development and implementation of an ecumenical mind has been painfully absent from most of the churches, even those which are officially devoted to the cause. It is almost as if the churches were hoping the whole subject would go away. This attitude is most noticeable within the ranks of the churches with a more cautious theological stance. There, instead of an ecumenical commitment being evidenced, we discern a policy which seems to hold that the less said about ecumenism, the better. Churches in the 1960s do not indulge in the kind of polemics which characterized an earlier day, but neither do they say much official good about one another. Each of the churches pursues a course of polite silence with regard to the others.

While the churches ignore each other's existence, the people do not. Despite the lack of any clear directive, Protestant Christians frequently transfer membership from one church to another with little

[22] Quoted in Kennedy, p. 56.

[23] Cf. the Report of the Department of Faith and Order, *Evanston to New Delhi*, pp. 40 ff.

[24] Bilheimer, p. 110.

apparent discomfort. "I never could see that the differences really mattered," they explain. So upon moving to a new home, which the average American does once every 5 years, a Protestant Christian is likely to join the nearest church or the one whose minister appeals to him the most. In only a minority of cases does "denominational loyalty" influence individual Christians to seek out a parish of the church from whence they came if any substantial sacrifice in time and effort is required to get to it.

The emergence of "ecumenism made easy," or "every man his own ecumenical movement," received the attention of several sections at the Oberlin Conference, with only uncertain results. The section on The Variations in Denominational Polities reported:

> . . . though the easy mobility of both clergy and laity from one church to another in North America may be interpreted as meaning that matters of faith and order are not, after all, of basic importance, yet its deeper import may be that such mobility reflects a kind of American dilution of the Christian faith into "religion in general" and the assumption that personal feelings of "natural piety" and "the good life" are quite sufficient, though we would not deny that some mobility may well represent the conviction that the really primary Christian tradition underlies all our particular traditions.[25]

It is obvious that the conferees were uncomfortable, even as the churches are uncomfortable, upon realizing how loosely the people sit to denominational loyalties. All of this is an urgent reason for the churches to begin a radical facing of the ecumenical question or risk having the majority of the membership solve it on terms that often do less than justice to the Gospel. Authentic ecumenism is rooted in Christ, not convenience. To the extent that the churches are renewed and grow together in the Gospel, the rapid turnover in the churches will be kept from being an example of a mere commitment to religion in general.

There is a further reason for the churches to address themselves to the problem of developing an ecumenical mind, so far as they are able. Increasingly the churches are encountering situations where it is not only undesirable but impossible for them to act alone. In the fall of 1964 a congregation was formed in a small town of declining population in rural Pennsylvania. The congregation was created out of the remnants of four churches of as many denominations. Together the churches constituted a strong parish. Singly they could afford

[25] In Minear, p. 238.

only minimal congregational programs or none at all. The launching of the new congregation was attended with ceremonies befitting its unusual origin, with dignitaries from the various denominations represented in the new church taking part. First reports indicate that the congregation is doing well.

Despite the press notices and mutual congratulations, it is difficult to avoid the conclusion that the new congregation represents little more than ecumenism by bankruptcy. It may be that the churches will finally resort to such a device when all is lost, but surely no one will argue that this is the ideal way for unity to be advanced. If we acquiesce to some form of a united church when the situation is so clamant that we cannot do anything else, it would seem reasonable for us to devote more attention to the things that make for unity when our circumstances are more prosperous. We know now that to maintain the presence of the church, we will accede to some united action, certain requirements having been met. It ought to be possible for us to read the implications of that strategy back into the life of our churches today.

An ecumenical mind is a gift to be prayed for. Like other gifts of God its bestowal might have surprising, even disconcerting results. He who shares the ecumenical mind must live in the tension between a love for the particular church which has given him his faith and the one church of Jesus Christ. The closer we involve ourselves with Christians in churches other than our own, the more we shall be faced with the task of being brothers to them with all that this implies. Because unity is inextricably bound up with truth, authentic ecumenism might at times force us to say No when we would wish to say Yes to our brethren. Finally, an ecumenical mind must be open to all the possibilities, both painful and glorious, that God has in store for the church as she presses onward to the end.

We have not attempted to describe in specific terms what a consistent attention to ecumenism might mean for the empirical life of the churches. Each church must discover this for itself on the basis of its own traditions and convictions. An ecumenical mind in the churches, however, will force the churches to view all that they do in a new light. It will lead them to make the great words of New Delhi immediately their own:

> We must seek together the fullness of Christian unity. We need for
> this purpose every member of the Christian family, of Eastern and

Western tradition, ancient churches and younger churches, men and women, young and old, of every race and every nation. Our brethren in Christ are given to us, not chosen by us. In some things our convictions do not yet permit us to act together, but we have made progress in giving content to the unity we seek. *Let us everywhere find out the things which in each place we can do together now; and faithfully do them,* praying and working always for that fuller unity which Christ wills for His Church.[26]

[26] Quoted in Kennedy, p. 69.

Bibliography of Caemmerer

Books and Papers

PUBLISHED VOLUMES

The Atoning Christ. New York: Ernst Kaufmann, 1947.

The Church in the World. St. Louis: Concordia Publishing House, 1949;
third printing, revised bibliography, 1961.

The Cross for Every Day (with Jaroslav J. Pelikan). Concordia, 1952.

Preaching for the Church. Concordia, 1959.

Lectures on Deuteronomy (trans.), *Luther's Works,* American Edition, Vol. 9.
Concordia, 1960.

God's Great Plan for You. Concordia, 1961.

Feeding and Leading. Concordia, 1962.

Christ Builds His Church. Concordia, 1963.

COMPONENTS IN PUBLISHED VOLUMES

Lutheran Book of Prayer. Concordia, 1940.

"The Christian Family — a Living Force in the Modern World,"
*The Christian Family in the Modern World: Fifth Yearbook of the Lu-
theran Education Association,* ed. Walter F. Wolbrecht. River Forest,
Ill., 1948.

"Temptation" and "The Nature of God," *The Abiding Word,* Vol. II. Concordia, 1947.

"The Fifth Sunday After Epiphany," *Sermonic Studies,* Vol. I. Concordia,
1957.

"The Human Family in God's Design," *Helping Families Through the Church,*
ed. Oscar E. Feucht. Concordia, 1957.

"Church Unity and Communication," *Christian Unity in North America,* ed. J. Robert Nelson. St. Louis: Bethany, 1958.

"The Practice of Holy Communion," *The Abiding Word,* Vol. III. Concordia, 1960.

"The Pastor at Work" and "The Pastor in the Pulpit," *The Pastor at Work.* Concordia, 1960.

"The Twenty-Second Sunday After Trinity," *Sermonic Studies,* Vol. II. Concordia, 1963.

"The Ministry of the Word," *Theology in the Life of the Church,* ed. Robert W. Bertram. Philadelphia: Fortress Press, 1963.

"The Church in the New Testament" and "Ministry in the New Testament," *Church and Ministry in Transition,* ed. Erwin L. Lueker. Concordia, 1964.

Foreword in *Toward a More Excellent Ministry* (ed. with A. O. Fuerbringer). Concordia, 1964.

CONTRIBUTIONS IN PUBLISHED PROCEEDINGS

Conventions of Districts, The Lutheran Church — Missouri Synod

Atlantic, Bronxville, 1942: "The Lutheran Church Faces the World."

North Dakota, Bismarck, 1946: "Temptation" (see above, *The Abiding Word*).

California and Nevada, Lodi, 1946, and Southern California, Anaheim, 1946: "The Nature of God" (see above, *The Abiding Word*).

Northwest, 1948: "The Church in the World" (see title above).

Western, St. Louis, 1951: "The Christian Family in the Modern World."

English, River Forest, 1954: "Church and State."

Central Illinois, Springfield, 1954: "The Visible and Invisible Church."

Colorado, Estes Park, 1955: "The Practice of Holy Communion" (see above, *The Abiding Word*).

Atlantic, Bronxville, 1958: "The Body of Christ."

Southeastern, Conover, 1960: "The Bible and the Word of God." Florida-Georgia, St. Petersburg, 1961: "The Bible and the Word of God."

Eastern, Pittsburgh, 1963: "God's Word for His People."

Texas, Austin, 1964: "Let the Church Be the Church."

Conventions of Associated Lutheran Charities

September 1946 (Annual Social Work Institute), Valparaiso: "The Application of Christian Ethics to Current Social Problems."

September 1948, Chicago: "Lutheran Social Action."

September 1949, St. Louis: "Luther's Concept of Welfare Work."

Valparaiso University

Institute on Race Relations, 1951: "Race Relations — the Christian Directive."

Church Music Seminar: "The Congregational Hymn as the Living Voice of the Gospel." Published in *The Musical Heritage of the Lutheran Church,* Vol. V. Concordia, 1959.

Institute on the Church and Modern Culture, 1953: "The Contributions of Lutheranism to Education, with Special Reference to Germany and the Scandinavian Countries."

Consultation on Law and Theology, 1960: "The Natural Law — A Theologian's View." Published by Lutheran Academy for Scholarship. Saint Louis, 1961.

Institute on Race Relations, 1963: "Free Indeed — Through Christ." Published in *The Roots.* Valparaiso, Ind.

National Lutheran Council, Church in Town and Country, Seminar 1964: "Outdoor Leisure."

National Lutheran Educational Conference, St. Louis, 1965: "The Concept of the Church and the Church's Educational Institutions."

ARTICLES IN PUBLICATIONS

Concordia Theological Monthly

"The Dynamic of the Lutheran Reformation," I, 8 (August 1930).

"On Liturgical Uniformity," IX, 6 (June 1938).

"The Melanchthonian Blight," XVIII, 5 (May 1947).

"Lutheran Preaching and Its Relation to the Audience," XVIII, 12 (December 1947).

"The Universal Priesthood and the Pastor," XIX, 8 (August 1948).

"The Christian Pastor and Courtesy," XX, 7 (July 1949).

"God's Grace the Preacher's Tool," XXI, 2 (February 1950).

"A Concordance Study of the Concept 'Word of God,'" XXII, 3 (March 1951).

"Give Attendance to Reading," XXIII, 9 (September 1952).

"Training the Parish for Christian Citizenship," XXIV, 10 (October 1953).

"The Educational Use of Scripture in the Light of the Doctrine of the Holy Spirit," XXVIII, 3 (March 1957).

"Preaching in Lent," XXXI, 1 (January 1960).

"Kerygma and Didache in Christian Education," XXXII, 4 (April 1961).

"Investment for Eternity," XXXIV, 2 (February 1963).

"The Body of Christ," XXV, 5 (May 1964).

Lutheran Education

"The Spiritual Life of the Teacher," XCV, 2 (October 1959).

"Legalism and the Gospel in Christian Education," XCVI, 5 (January 1961).

"Revivalism and the Gospel in Christian Education," XCVI, 6 (February 1961).

"Theological Foundations for the Religion Curriculum in the Lutheran School," C, 1 (September, 1964).

The Christian Century

"Church Unity and Communication," LXXIII, 14 (April 4, 1956) (see above, *Christian Unity in North America*)

"The Atonement — As Divine Initiative," LXXVIII, 42 (Oct. 18, 1961).

The Lutheran Scholar

"The First Lutheran Scholar," III, 2 (April 1946).

The Lutheran Quarterly

"The Office of Overseer in the Church," VIII, I (February 1956).

Una Sancta

"Preaching from Easter to Pentecost," XIX, 2 (Easter 1962).

The American Lutheran

"What Is Lutheran in Faith and Life?" XLVII, 4 (April 1964).

The Seminarian, St. Louis, Missouri

"Luther and the Living Word," XLI, 5 (Jan. 25, 1950).

"The Word of God," XLII, 5 (Jan. 24, 1951).

"Man, God, and Society," XLIII, 6 (Feb. 20, 1952).

"Preaching from the Old Testament," XLV, 10 (June 2, 1954)

"The Ministry Is Ministry," L, 4 (May 1959).

Other articles in *The Cresset, The Lutheran Witness, The Walther League Messenger, Interaction.*

MAJOR UNPUBLISHED PAPERS: PREACHING AND PASTORATE

"The Office and Calling of the Lutheran Minister in the 20th Century," Detroit Pastoral Conference, The Lutheran Church — Missouri Synod, 1945.

"The Pastor's Growth," Detroit Pastors Conference, 1950.

"Preaching the Gospel to Christians: I. The Purpose, II. The Method, III. The Helps," South Central District, ELC, 1952.

"The Relation of the Sermon to the Liturgy," Northwest Pastoral Conference of the English District, 1954.

"Craftsmanship in Preaching: I. In Proclamation, II. In Worship, III. In Planning," Passavant Lectures, Chicago Lutheran Seminary at Maywood, 1955.

"Preaching," 3 units, Pastoral Retreat, California District, ELC, 1956.

"Preaching Christ: I. For Faith, II. For Life, III. For the Body," Gullixson Lectures, Luther Seminary Convocation, 1957.

"Christian Ethics as They Apply to Our Relationship with Other Lutherans and Protestants," Erie Pastoral Conference, English District, 1959.

"The Dynamics of Preaching: I. For Renewal, II. For Meaning, III. For Communication," Central Lutheran Seminary, 1960 Pre-Lenten Lectures.

"God's Word to People: I. See the People in the Text, II. Remember the People in the Process, III. Express the People in Words, IV. Reach the People in Speech," Luther Theological Seminary, Saskatoon, 1961.

"Effective Preaching," Central Illinois District Pastoral Conference, 1961.

"The Word Through Preaching," Anniversary Convention, English District, 1961.

"Remaining Stable in a Period of Transition," Central Pastoral Conference, Southern Illinois District, 1962.

"The Church and Its Practical Dimensions: I. The Premises, II. The Church in the Parish, III. The Church Throughout the World," Southern District Pastoral Conference, 1962.

"Preaching in Institutions: I. The Meaning of Preaching, II. Preaching in Institutions," Chaplain Workshop, Concordia Seminary, St. Louis, 1964.

"The Preacher and the Power of the Gospel: I. For Reality, II. For Fellowship, III. For Refreshment," Pastoral Conference, Illinois Synod, LCA, 1964.

"The Church and the Local Congregation: I. The Congregation Functioning as the Church, II. The Pastorate in That Congregation," English District Pastoral Conference, St. Louis, 1964.

"Current Biblical Accents and Preaching: I. The New Hermeneutic, II. The Meaning of Words, III. The Rediscovery of the Church," Pastoral Institute, Concordia Senior College, 1965.

MAJOR UNPUBLISHED PAPERS, MISCELLANEOUS TOPICS

"The Relevance of Fundamental Christian Thinking to the Problem of American Life Today."

"The Mature Christian."

"The Church and the Natural Order," Institute on Social Problems, Lutheran Students Association, University of Illinois, 1945.

"The Basic Motives of Christian Ethics in Action," Lutheran Academy for Scholarship, 1946.

"The Word in the Church of the Reformation," New England Lutheran Faculty Conference, 1958.

"Christian Discipline in a Lutheran School," High School Teachers Conference, 1959; reissued by LCMS Board for Higher Education, 1960.

"The Doctrine of Justification in Early Lutheran and Contemporary Theologies," Alumni Institute, St. Louis, 1963.

"The Objectives and Role of Communication in the Internal Life of the Church," Lutheran Communications Conference, St. Louis, 1963. Adapted in *Interaction*.

"The Preaching of the Gospel"; "The Faith That Goes Forward"; "Faith Forward — Of Pastor and Teacher"; "Faith Forward — In the Worshiping Fellowship"; "Faith Forward — In the Self-Sacrificing Fellowship," Oklahoma District, LCMS, Pastors and Teachers Conference, October 1963.

"The Gospel in Speaking and Writing," Workshop of Commission on Church Literature, St. Louis, 1964.

"Called to be Servants of the Word in the World," Episcopal Convention Ecumenical Day, Eden Seminary unit, 1964.

Contributors

Robert W. Bertram, Associate Professor of Historical and Systematic Theology, Concordia Seminary, St. Louis, Missouri

Richard R. Caemmerer, Sr., Professor of Homiletics and Dean of the Chapel, Concordia Seminary, St. Louis, Missouri

Richard R. Caemmerer, Jr., Assistant Professor of Art, Valparaiso University, Valparaiso, Indiana

John H. Elliott, Assistant Professor of Exegetical Theology, Concordia Seminary, St. Louis, Missouri

Paul W. Harms, Associate Professor of English and Speech, Concordia Senior College, Fort Wayne, Indiana

Robert T. Hoeferkamp, Associate Professor of Theology, Centro de Estudios Teologicos Augsburgo, Mexico City, Mexico

Richard E. Koenig, Pastor, Immanuel Lutheran Church, Amherst, Massachusetts

Kenneth F. Korby, Assistant Professor of Theology, Valparaiso University, Valparaiso, Indiana

F. Dean Lueking, Pastor, Grace Lutheran Church, River Forest, Illinois

Martin E. Marty, Associate Professor of Church History, The Divinity School, The University of Chicago, and Associate Editor of *The Christian Century*

Edward H. Schroeder, Associate Professor of Theology, Valparaiso University, Valparaiso, Indiana

David S. Schuller, Associate Professor of Homiletics and Pastoral Theology, Concordia Seminary, St. Louis, Missouri

Robert C. Schultz, Pastor, St. Paul Lutheran Church, Bayonne, New Jersey.

Jaroslav J. Vajda, Editor of *This Day,* St. Louis, Missouri